The Fanaticism of the Apocalypse

To my children, Eric and Anna,
who have given me such joy

The Fanaticism of the Apocalypse

Save the Earth, Punish Human Beings

Pascal Bruckner

Translated by
Steven Rendall

polity

First published in French as *Le fanaticisme de l'Apocalypse* © Éditions Grasset & Fasquelle, 2011.

This English edition © Polity Press, 2013

Polity Press
65 Bridge Street
Cambridge CB2 1UR, UK

Polity Press
350 Main Street
Malden, MA 02148, USA

ISBN-13: 978-0-7456-6976-2

A catalogue record for this book is available from the British Library.

Typeset in 11 on 13 pt Sabon
by Toppan Best-set Premedia Limited
Printed and bound in Great Britain by the MPG Printgroup

The publisher has used its best endeavours to ensure that the URLs for external websites referred to in this book are correct and active at the time of going to press. However, the publisher has no responsibility for the websites and can make no guarantee that a site will remain live or that the content is or will remain appropriate.

Every effort has been made to trace all copyright holders, but if any have been inadvertently overlooked the publisher will be pleased to include any necessary credits in any subsequent reprint or edition.

For further information on Polity, visit our website: www.politybooks.com

Contents

The world will come to an end. The only reason it might last is that it exists. How weak this reason is compared to all those that herald the contrary [...] we will perish for the very reason we thought we would live. Machinery will have Americanized us so much and progress will have so fully atrophied our spiritual side that nothing in the utopians' bloody, sacrilegious or anti-natural dreams will be comparable to its positive results.

Baudelaire, Fusées

Why make us fear our lives?

Voltaire, contra Pascal

Introduction

The Return of Original Sin

In Jesuit schools we were urged to strengthen our faith by spending time in monasteries. We were assigned spiritual exercises to be dutifully written in little notebooks that were supposed to renew the promises made at baptism and to celebrate the virtues of Christian love and succour for the weak. It wasn't enough just to believe; we had to testify to our adhesion to the Holy Scriptures and drive Satan out of our hearts. These practices were sanctioned by daily confessions under the guidance of a priest. We all probed our hearts to extirpate the germs of iniquity and to test, with a delicious thrill, the borderline separating grace from sin. We were immersed in an atmosphere of meditative reverence, and the desire to be good gave our days a special contour. We knew that God was looking down on us indulgently: we were young, we were allowed to stumble. In his great ledger, he wrote down each of our actions, weighing them with perfect equanimity. We engaged in refined forms of piety in order to gain favours. Regarded from an adult point of view, these childish efforts, which were close to the ancients' spiritual exercises, were not without a certain nobility. They wavered between

docility and a feeling of lofty grandeur. At least we
learned the art of knowing ourselves, of resisting the
turmoil of puberty.

What a surprise to witness, half a century later and
in an agnostic society, the powerful return of this frame
of mind, but this time under the aegis of science. Consider the meaning in contemporary jargon of the famous
carbon footprint that we all leave behind us. What is it,
after all, if not the gaseous equivalent of Original Sin,
of the stain that we inflict on our Mother Gaia by the
simple fact of being present and breathing? We can all
gauge the volume of our emissions, day after day, with
the injunction to curtail them, just as children saying
their catechisms are supposed to curtail their sins.
Human beings are held responsible for all the damage
they inflict on their habitat. A change of scale: alongside
the oppressed and the humiliated with whom we are
already familiar, a new figure makes its entry on the
stage of History: the Earth. Our task is to prevent this
cradle from becoming our collective coffin.

Ecologism, the sole truly original force of the past
half-century, has challenged the goals of progress and
raised the question of its limits. It has awakened our
sensitivity to nature, emphasized the effects of climate
change, pointed out the exhaustion of fossil fuels. Onto
this collective credo has been grafted a whole apocalyptic scenography that has already been tried out with
communism, and that borrows from Gnosticism as
much as from medieval forms of messianism. Cataclysm
is part of the basic tool-kit of Green critical analysis,
and prophets of decay and decomposition abound. They
constantly beat the drums of panic and call upon us to
expiate our sins before it is too late.

This fear of the future, of science, and of technology
reflects a time when humanity, and especially Western
humanity, has taken a sudden dislike to itself. We are
exasperated by our own proliferation, and can no longer
stand ourselves. Whether we want to be or not, we are

tangled up with seven billion other members of our species. Rejecting both capitalism and socialism, ecologism has come to power nowhere (except in one German *Land*) and has never shed blood, at least not up to now. But it has won the battle of ideas. Taking advantage of the failure of its predecessors – Marxism, Third-Worldism – it is triumphant, by capillary action, at the UN, in governments, in schools. It has become the dominant temper of the dawn of the twenty-first century. It excels more in preventing than in proposing: it closes factories, blocks projects, forbids the construction of super-highways, airports, railway lines. It is the power that always denies. Where it has become a political force, it always breaks up into cliques or factions that hate each other and fall prey to the narcissism of small differences: the greater the complicity, the more bitter the hostility. Here as elsewhere, it is always the most vehement who win out, inflecting doctrine toward the extreme. The environment is the new secular religion that is rising, in Europe at least, from the ruins of a disbelieving world. We have to subject it to critical evaluation in turn and unmask the infantile disease that is eroding and discrediting it: catastrophism.

There are at least two ecologies: one rational, the other nonsensical; one that broadens our outlook while the other narrows it; one democratic, the other totalitarian. The first wants to tell us about the damage done by industrial civilization; the second deduces from this the human species' guilt. For the latter, nature is only a stick to be used to beat human beings. Just as Third-Worldism was the shame of colonial history, and repentance was contrition with regard to the present,[1] catastrophism constitutes the anticipated remorse of the future: the meaning of history having evaporated, every change is a potential collapse that augurs nothing good. Its favourite mode of expression is accusation: revolutionaries wanted to erase the past and start over from zero; now the focus is on condemning past and present wrongs and bringing them before the tribunal of public opinion. The eighteenth century had acquitted human beings and declared them innocent; we are reopening old cases, reactivating all the indictments. Now no leniency is possible; our crime has been calculated in terms of devastated forests, burned-over lands, and extinct species, and it has entered the pitiless domain of statistics. The wrong no longer proceeds from nature, from political or religious fanaticism; it is born of the Promethean ambition of the individual who has ravaged the planet. The recent history of Western culture is nothing less than the simultaneous piling up of forms of guilt and liberation: we emancipate, on one hand, in order to lock up, on the other; we destroy taboos only in order to forge new ones. Prohibition shifts to a new object but never disappears.

The prevailing anxiety is at once a recognition of real problems and a symptom of the ageing of the West, a reflection of its psychic fatigue. Our pathos is that of the end of time. And because no one ever thinks alone, because the spirit of an age is always a collective worker, it is tempting to give oneself up to this gloomy tide. Or, on the contrary, we could wake up from this nightmare and rid ourselves of it.

Part I

The Seductive Attraction of Disaster

1

Give Me Back My Enemy

We all live in a house on fire, no fire department to call;
no way out, just the upstairs window to look out of
while the fire burns the house down with us trapped,
locked in it.

Tennessee Williams

O God, show me the enemy. Once you find out who the
enemy is, you can kill him. But these people here they
confuse me. Who hurt me? Who spoil my life? Tell me
who to beat back.

V.S. Naipaul

It happened in 1989, and that seems centuries ago. The
world was emerging from the Cold War; the USSR,
exhausted, was allowing subject peoples to escape its
rule and preparing for its transition to a market economy.
Euphoria reigned: Western civilization had just won by
a knockout, without having had to go to war. Twice, in
the course of the past century, it had triumphed over its
worst opponents, fascism and communism, two illegiti-
mate children to which it had given birth and which it
was able to suffocate. At that time, anyone who
expressed reservations or emphasized that it was less a

victory of capitalism than a defeat of communism was accused of being a killjoy.

Farewell to insouciance

However, at the very moment when the Soviet system was playing a nasty trick on us by bowing out, enthusiasm was vying with fear: an adversary is a security against the future, a permanent competitor who forces us to reshape ourselves. Though we can never be sure of the affection of those closest to us, we can always count on the hatred of our enemies. They are the guarantors of our existence, they allow us to know who we are. Their aversion is almost a form of homage. Not to inspire any antipathy is to enjoy the tranquillity of the insignificant.

The East–West conflict provided meaning: it tore out of inertia peoples only too willing to sink into the delights of abundance. It maintained the clearness of a world divided into two identifiable camps. Communism's ambition was to do away with bourgeois democracies as a whole, to put an end to the exploitation of other human beings, to invent a new mode of production that would consign earlier societies to pre-history. From biology to philosophy, there was no discipline that remained unaffected by communism or was not convinced that it was working on an unprecedented anthropological type.

> [Under communism] Man will become immeasurably stronger, wiser and subtler; his body will become more harmonized, his movements more rhythmic, his voice more musical. The forms of life will become dynamically dramatic. The average human type will rise to the heights of an Aristotle, a Goethe, or a Marx. And above this ridge new peaks will rise. (Leon Trotsky, *Literature and Revolution*, 1924)

The implosion of the Soviet Union worried us as much as it flattered us: being the sole winner in a conflict means concentrating on oneself all the criticism that could earlier be deflected onto others. Communism had bit the dust but capitalism would soon regret having killed it. Left alone on the field, capitalism now weighs on the planet's fate like a *fatum*: it is not credited with any good deed, but it is held responsible for all harms.

It failed in the West with the economic crisis of 2008, at the very moment that its logic had been adopted by most nations. A world that lives on credit – the United States and Europe – is confronted by a world that lives on borrowed time – China, India, and Brazil – and works hard, without a social safety net, in order to emerge from misery. By a terrible irony that reminds us of the Hegelian master–slave dialectic, it is these poor countries that are becoming the rich countries' creditors, renegotiating their debts, flooding their markets, and buying up their companies – or even their heritages, as in the case of Greece, whose beaches, archaeological sites, ports, and fleet are up for sale. Thus we find opposed the two ages of capitalism: that of asceticism among the emerging countries, and that of hedonism in the West, with the fear that the former might make the latter dependent on them. A bitter victory: at least in the West, we see the market economy prey to an uncontrollable chaos, as if it were about to die after the death of its old rival. In a way, the Soviet Union maintained our immune system, while victory threatens to leave us defenceless.[1] All the more because deregulating the market also gives free rein to its worst vices, such as greed, the founding virtue in the liberal economics that maintains that private vices combine to produce the harmony of the whole. But over the past three decades, and especially with the financial revolution in the United States, this appetite for lucre has grown to dizzying heights, deepening inequalities and leading to a potential proletarianization of the middle classes.

What was the real estate boom of 2008 if not the consequence of an impossible equation: allowing salaried workers access to property without increasing their incomes, thus saddling them with unreasonable debts? A minority of CEOs, bankers, and traders saw their wealth increase enormously while workers, employees, and lower-level managers accumulated mountains of loans until they went bankrupt. Even though it accompanied the Internet revolution, the liberal turning point inaugurated by Thatcher and Reagan in the name of the battle against taxes also constituted a neo-feudalism for the rich, who co-opted and helped each other to accumulate gigantic resources independently of any merit or result. In this way, those who lauded capitalism violated one of its most elementary laws, namely competition and the obligation to succeed.

The candidates for a successor

Who will claim, as communism did, to substitute another system for our values? Who will challenge us on such a large scale? Fundamentalist Islam? Even if it is gaining ground in many countries, accompanying the growth of a secular mentality like its shadow, it is directed primarily against Muslims themselves, whom it considers lukewarm and complicit with the modern world. Terrorism? Still alive and kicking, despite Bin Laden's death, and divided into franchises in Africa, the Near East, and Central Asia, since 11 September 2001 it has lost its lustre by becoming part of the mental landscape of everyday life. It is one of the threats that everyone has to take into account since any madman wearing an explosive belt can massacre dozens of people in a crowd or on a bus. There are useful enemies that make you fertile and sterile enemies that wear you out. Islamic terrorism is a cancer that teaches us nothing except paranoia. Combined with the work of the secret

services and the police, sang-froid and prudence are the
best responses to the bombers' barbarity. The French
have been living with this risk, which has become part
of their routine, for almost thirty years. Those who had
hoped, like American Republicans and Democrats, that
September 11 would be the symbolic equivalent of
Pearl Harbor and administer a healthy jolt to a people
immersed in its selfish comfort were disappointed, even
if governments have used this danger as a pretext for
imposing a state of emergency and restricting fundamental freedoms.[2]

It is difficult to reconstruct a credible adversary that
is dispersed to the four corners of the earth and that can
have all sorts of faces. We have to go further, to the
roots of the problem. And the problem is our aggressiveness, our relentless attack on nature. We are told by
Michel Serres, for example, that people stupidly fight
each other without realizing that the real battle is not
where they think it is. We are like the duellists in one
of Goya's paintings who are fencing on shifting sands
into which they are gradually sinking. We squabble with
one another while missing the essential point: the fate
of the material world that we are destroying by our little
schemes. For centuries, we have waged war on the
world by trying to dominate it; now we have to wage
war on war, sign an armistice with water, trees, stones,
the oceans.

> The damage we have inflicted up to now on the world
> is equivalent to the ravages that a world war would have
> left behind it. Our peacetime economic relationships are
> arriving, continuously and slowly, at the same results
> that a short, global conflict would produce, as if war no
> longer belonged to soldiers alone [. . .] We so-called
> developed nations are not fighting among ourselves
> anymore, we are all turning against the world. This is
> a war that is literally a world war, and twice over,
> because everyone, in the sense of human beings, is
> inflicting losses on the world, in the sense of things.[3]

We are behaving like parasites that destroy their host by invading it. In 2009, didn't the Swiss Greens and Socialists demand the dissolution of the Swiss army, which had become useless, since the true danger is global warming?

A strange observation: the more the Earth shrinks and is unified by means of communication and technology, the less we control its course. A dispossession through proximity. Weapons of mass destruction, whether atomic, biological, or chemical, put humanity in the situation of someone who lives with a gun to his head but is not free to restrain the finger on the trigger. At any moment, a nuclear holocaust set off by the madness of some Doctor Strangelove could eliminate hundreds of millions of people, and permanently destroy whole continents. The human race is a species whose obsolescence is programmed, according to the German philosopher Günther Anders, the husband of Hannah Arendt and a long-time opponent of atomic energy. 'We have entered into the end-times.' The global village is becoming the sum of the constraints that enslave all people to a single exteriority from which they are trying to save themselves. An implacable determinism that makes every individual the hostage of all others: the more the media, commerce, and trade bring continents and cultures closer together, the more the pressure becomes unbearable. The net is closing, eliciting a feeling of claustrophobia and a desire to escape to distant places or to colonize other planets. The human tribes never cease to overlap each other, leading in turn to a violent desire for separation and boundaries. We are no longer connected because we are no longer separated: we lack the distance to be able to communicate, the depth to be able to sympathize with each other. On a planet over which seven billion people will soon be swarming; isolation, slowness, calm, and contemplation are becoming once again luxuries for the few who are prepared to pay fortunes for them.

How can this malaise be transformed into a justified anger, how can its target be identified? By designating human beings as the danger *par excellence*. Rousseau already did so, contrary to all the optimism of the Enlightenment: 'Man, seek no longer the cause of the evil; you yourself are the cause. There is no evil other than the evil you do or suffer, and both of them come from you (*Émile*).' Numerous authors tell us that humanity as a whole has gone off-course, and that it has to be understood as an illness that must be immediately treated: 'Man is a cancer on the Earth [. . .] a throwaway species, like the civilization he invented.'[4] And Nicolas Hulot writes: 'The enemy does not come from outside, it resides within our system and our consciousnesses.'[5]

For the past half-century we have in fact been witnessing a slide from one scapegoat to another: Marxism designated capitalism as responsible for human misery. Third-Worldism, upset by the bourgeoisification of the working classes, substituted the West for capitalism as the great criminal in History and the 'inventor' of slavery, colonialism, and imperialism. 'Alterglobalism', which was more ephemeral, limited itself to combining its two predecessors. With ecologism, we move up a notch: the guilty party is humanity itself, in its will to dominate the planet, to 'challenge it' (*herausfordern*), to use Heidegger's terminology. Here there is a return to the fundamentals of Christianity: evil is the pride of the creatures who are in revolt against their Creator and who exceed their prerogatives. The three scapegoats can be cumulated: ecologism can reject the capitalism invented by a West that preys on peoples and is destroying the Earth. It is a system of Russian dolls that fit one inside the other until the final synthesis is reached. That is why so many old Bolsheviks are converting to ecologism in order to broaden their palette of accusations. This amounts to recycling anti-capitalist clichés as one recycles waste water: ecologism adds a supplementary layer of reprobation, claiming to be the culmination of all earlier critiques. Thus a whole segment of the South American left has seized upon this hobby-horse to reinforce its credo: 'There are only two solutions: either capitalism dies, or Mother Earth dies,' said Evo Morales, the president of Bolivia, in 2009. The globe becomes the new proletarian that has to be saved from exploitation, if need be by reducing the human population to 500 million, as Jacques Cousteau demanded,[6] and as some opponents of 'speciesism' also proclaim.[7] Human beings, a harmful and invasive race, could be eliminated without difficulty: '[I]f we were to take the standpoint of the Life Community and give voice to its true interest, the end of the human epoch on Earth would most likely be greeted with a hearty "Good riddance!"'[8] A delicious phrase if ever there was one: just imagine whales, trees, and carrots applauding the elimination of human beings! Even in his metaphors, Paul Taylor remains hopelessly anthropocentric. The same intention animates the Voluntary Human Extinction Movement (VHEMT), a group of individuals who have decided not to reproduce themselves:

> Each time another one of us decides to not add another one of us to the burgeoning millions already squatting on this ravaged planet, another ray of hope shines through the gloom. When every human chooses to stop breeding, Earth's biosphere will be allowed to return to its former glory.[9]

In the nineteenth century, the French historian Hippolyte Taine already said, 'I love my children too much to give them life.' Even the bio-geographer Jared Diamond, who has written a magisterial study of the disappearance of societies, gives voice to a strange dream: 'If most of the world's 6 billion people today were in cryogenic storage and neither eating, breathing, nor metabolizing, that large population would cause no environmental problems.'[10]

An artificial coma as a solution to the planet's problems. What is ecologism? A real estate squabble in an overpopulated apartment building. The planet is too small and we are too numerous. Throw them out! According to James Lovelock, who trained as a chemist, the Earth is an animate organism constituted of multiple cells in an unstable equilibrium. In this conglomeration, human beings behave like cancerous metastases, proliferating at the expense of the whole, which rejects and expels them as useless grafts. In short, *Homo sapiens* is nothing other than *Homo demens*. In France, Yves Cochet, a Green Party politician who is a member of the European Parliament, proposed on 6 April 2009 that couples who conceived a third child should be penalized, on the ground that a baby is equivalent, in terms of pollution, to 620 roundtrips by air between Paris and New York.

The offence against Gaia

The despondency of European nations is striking, given that our lives are still extraordinarily pleasant: everywhere the culture of lament prevails. Not only does every minority seek to obtain the title of pariah, but every citizen, at some time or another, seeks to don the rags of the persecuted wretch in order to put the spotlight on him- or herself. The fine insouciance of the post-war period is forgotten; the happy days are behind us. We have to have grave expressions on our faces, and wrinkle our brows: the perils are so numerous that we can hardly choose among them. Sounding the death knell is our *viaticum*. Saving the world requires us to denigrate everything that has to do with the spirit of enterprise and the taste for discovery, especially in the field of science. We have ceased to admire; we know only how to denounce, decry, whine. The capacity for enthusiasm is dying out.

That is because at the turn of the twenty-first century a paradigm change took place: we passed from the age of revolutions to the 'age of catastrophes'.[11] The first age still assumed a horizon of expectation, a precise actor capable of drawing the human species along after it. As soon as the end of history was sounded, at least in the West, the idea of progress was in its death throes and time curled up on itself and abandoned its dimension of projection. It is no longer anything but a precipitate of misfortunes. The future of the world as a material totality predominates over the world of human societies to come. The long list of emblematic victims – Jews, Blacks, slaves, proletarians, colonized peoples – is gradually replaced by the Planet, which has become the paragon of all the wretched. It is the absolute outcast. 'The Earth is moved,' Michel Serres writes, retranslating the famous phrase 'E pur si muove' that Galileo muttered in 1633 when the Inquisition had forced him to abjure his theory of heliocentrism.[12] In the convulsions of our Earth, that mineral and vegetable Christ, it is the immense cohort of the damned that cries out to us and demands justice. A fundamental shift: henceforth it is not a specific community that we are asked to identify with, but rather a small spaceship that carries us and groans. It is no longer a question of transforming the world but of preserving it. We nourish a melancholy vision of our lakes, our forests, our countrysides whose fragility overwhelms us and whose obliteration we seek to prevent. We see the whole globe as a perpetual autumn that relegates to the past the lovely summer of its blooming. Development bears within it only disintegration. The slightest accidents, oil spills, floods, heavy rains, and heat waves are the fateful harbingers of what awaits us.

An example? In 1947, a group of atomic scientists, concerned about the tension between the USA and the

USSR, constructed a Doomsday Clock whose little minute hand indicated the time separating us from the disaster to occur at midnight. The highpoint of the risk was reached in 1953, when Washington and Moscow both tested thermonuclear bombs within a nine-month period, and again in 1962, during the Cuban Missile Crisis. The clock, which has since been constantly updated, now also takes into account the threats posed by climate change and new technologies. In January 2010, for example, it located human destiny at less than six minutes from general annihilation. In this short interval, every second counts: we are at the edge of the precipice – that is what we are told by this instrument that revives the Christian terrors of the Last Days. Humanity is moving toward its conclusions; it is advisable to represent that fact symbolically in order to put us on guard against ourselves. 'The house is burning but we are looking elsewhere,' Jacques Chirac said in 2002 at the Johannesburg summit meeting, inviting the participants to invent 'a new relationship between man and nature'. Sir Martin Rees, an astrophysicist who holds the Isaac Newton chair at Cambridge, published a book with a resounding title – *Our Final Hour* – in which he gave humanity a 50 per cent chance of surviving the twenty-first century, because of its proliferation and its wicked inventions.[13] Yes, the end is near; we have to drop everything else and prepare ourselves.

It's too late, a British journalist warns us:

> Quietly in public, loudly in private, climate scientists everywhere are saying the same thing: it's over. The years in which more than two degrees of global warming could have been prevented have passed, the opportunities squandered by denial and delay. [. . .] Even if we were to cut carbon emissions to zero today, by the year 3000 our contribution to atmospheric concentrations would decline by just 40%.[14]

In a strange mixture of fatalism and activism to which Marxism had already accustomed us, a certain kind of ecologism describes the death of the planet as inexorable while at the same time exhorting us to delay it as much as we can. Not only are we experiencing the death of species at the frightening rate of fifty to two hundred a day – in the official discourse, it is the 'sixth extinction'[15] – and not only are the coral reefs in danger of disappearing between now and 2050, but according to oncologists and toxicologists, 'the end of humanity will probably arrive sooner than expected, around 2060, as a result of the generalized sterility of male sperm caused by pesticides and other persistent organic pollutants (POPs) and carcinogens, mutagens, and reprotoxics (CMR).' With an acceleration of natural disturbances, rising temperatures, and countless pandemics, 'We all know now that we are headed straight for disaster.'[16] The image of a race car running into a brick wall is one of the most common in this kind of literature, and another is the *Titanic*, the symbol of human arrogance sailing toward the iceberg that is going to send it to the bottom of the ocean. The *Titanic* or the anti-Noah's ark: whereas the prophet tried to save the human race from the Flood by taking along one pair of each species, the ocean liner casts it into the sea. The former's prudence saves him, the latter's mad pride dooms it. 'We know from our knowledge of the ancient past that if we continue our present growth path we are facing the end of civilization as we know it – not in millions of years, or even millennia, but by the end of this century.'[17]

The disappearance of the best and the persistence of the worst: that is what we are experiencing. In the meantime, biological diversity flickers out and glaciers melt while detritus and plastic bags pile up. The health of the planet? It is irremediably deteriorating because the ecological footprint exceeds 50 per cent of the Earth's capacity for regeneration, that is, for absorbing waste products and for reproducing resources. A mathematical miracle: humanity lives on credit at the Earth's expense and, like our Western economies, finds itself in a state of quasi-bankruptcy.

'In 2007 human beings used the equivalent of a planet and a half!'[18] Wow! the calculation is odd but striking. Here we are subject to a double-penalty system: to the colossal debt accumulated by the North and financed by the South in an incredible reversal of their respective situations we must add the latter's no less gigantic outstanding balance with regard to the planet. Seen from this point of view, the various cataclysms are only somewhat crude reminders of drafts to be honoured: In ten years, we were told by Al Gore in 2006,[19] we will no longer be able to reverse the process of the planet's deterioration, and our civilizations will have to move from denial to the recognition without which they will sink into despair.

This literature is proliferating and turning into clichés so much that similar quotations could be multiplied indefinitely. The litany of failure is endless. Ecologism has become a global ideology that covers all of existence, modes of production as much as ways of life. In it are found all the faults of Marxism applied to the environment: the omnipresent scientism, the appalling visions of reality, the admonishment of those who are guilty of not understanding those who wish them well. All the foolishness of Bolshevism, Maoism, and Trotskyism are somehow reformulated exponentially in the name of saving the planet. All these authors, journalists, politicians, and scientists compete in announcing the abominable and lay claim to a hyperlucidity: they alone see things correctly, whereas others vegetate in the slumber from which they will someday awaken, terrified. They alone have emerged from the cave of ignorance in which the human herd mills around, deaf and blind to the obvious. In 1979 the German philosopher Hans Jonas, a disciple of Heidegger and the Green Party's guru, already wrote in an otherwise impressive book that the industrial party was over, and that ethics had to be reformulated to take into account a new responsibility to the natural world.[20] The latter, faced with raging promethean technology that imposes orders of an entirely new magnitude, can no longer take care of itself and has to be saved, the way one saves a sick child. Otherwise the apocalypse will be inevitable. 'Our time is running out,' two professors warn us.[21] We are living our last hours. For example, in September 2010 the monthly *La Décroissance* asserted that: 'The enemies of life are found not only among the industrialists, but also those who do not believe in the catastrophe.'

So the catastrophe has to be not feared but believed in, the way others believe in God! It is a matter not of demonstration but of faith. We have to drop everything, suspend all human activities – as happened in April 2010, when a volcanic eruption in Iceland halted all air traffic over the North Atlantic, gladdening environmental activists, who were delighted to see huge airliners immobilized on the tarmac, airports closed, and businessmen and tourists punished for their travel mania by being stuck thousands of miles from their home countries. The hot ashes from the explosion gave rise to the sad passions of revenge and repentance. The question is not how to minimize the dangers that threaten us. Is that why so many intelligent people, so many brilliant minds among our government officials, scientists, and intellectuals, are beginning to reason, with the best intentions, like the most elementary Hollywood scenarios, such as *The Day After*, *Independence Day*, and *2012*?

The Car: The End of the Libido?

In 2008, right in the middle of the financial recession, thousands of new cars were lined up in parking lots and warehouses across Europe and

America, waiting in vain for buyers. These parking lots had nothing in common with the classic car graveyards, piles of crumpled metal rusting in the fields, as at the mythical Cadillac Ranch along Highway 66, metal monoliths stuck upright into the earth on the desolate plains near Amarillo, Texas. The latter testify to the vitality of an industry that left behind it a trail of waste products like so many monuments to its glory. The disaffection with the car, despite a rapidly expanding Asian market, is patent: everywhere, the big car companies are rethinking their production plans and turning toward hybrid or electric vehicles. A crisis for the fetish object that was the hero of the twentieth century and created so many masterpieces in its wake.

The car has long embodied a dream of autonomy: the freedom to move as we wish. For a world immersed in rural life, imprisoned within the confines of a village or a province, it seemed a miracle. Driving all night long, setting out on a whim, taking off for the unknown – that was and is the attraction of this home on wheels that incarnates one's individuality. The dream slowly collapsed as cities and roads became clogged: if all citizens have their own own vehicles, no one will be able to move, and the sleek sports car will become as slow as an ancient chariot. The car is increasingly immobilizing itself. Marvellous as long as it was reserved for a minority, it becomes a nightmare in urban traffic jams, expensive in terms of insurance, parking, traffic fines, and fuel. What is a privilege that is shared by everyone? A curse! The multiplying effect of demography makes the right to mobility obsolescent: when everyone wants to take a plane or a train at the same time, we end up waiting in crowded railway stations and airports, find beaches covered with people and tourist sites jammed. 'Democracy,' as Roberto Calasso has very nicely put it, is 'access for all to goods that no longer exist.' In half a century, the car, which used to be a symbol of liberation, has become a symbol of encumbrance and alienation. The intoxication of wide-open spaces has given way to a generalized coagulation. The end of the prestige connected with an aristocratic status.

It is not a question of going on a diet before indulging in an orgy; it is truly the conclusion of a cycle, at least in developed countries (in Japan, the number of car-owners has decreased by half). Starting in 2012, diesels and 4×4s, which are major emitters of particulates, are supposed to be banned in some French cities. The car manufacturers' last hope resides, as is well known, in the emergent countries, where all our illusions can still persist for a time. We will go on making cars – fourteen million a year in China alone, even though all its cities, like India's, are already saturated – but clean, plug-in electric cars, like the Tesla Roadster favoured by stars in California. Ride sharing will be widespread, and we will be able to rent cars by the hour or the day. We will all be 'responsible eco-citizens', as the current jargon has it; we will take the bus, the tram, scooters, or bicycles, and we will stop financing, by our gluttonous appetite for black gold, dictatorships and oppressive regimes. But what is a car that is not showy, polluting, or noisy? A means of transportation or of work, not an object of desire. This means the end of the ostentation of splendid convertibles whose luxury crushes ordinary people; the end of the exploits of lovers of speed who enjoy dizzying acceleration and flirt with death at every bend in the road. As long as the car was reserved for an elite, we could excuse and even admire the dreadful mutilations that it imposed on societies, and a fatal accident seemed like the inevitable tribute to be paid to its divinity. Reduced to a simple economic use, it loses, at least in cities, its symbolic glory.

Contrary to a popular cliché, the distances between various points on the globe have steadily increased: travel by train or aeroplane can stagnate in long queues to get through security. A strike, an incident, or a snowstorm can prolong your trip by several hours or even days. Travellers, always on edge, are amazed when they arrive safe and sound and on time. The withdrawal of the Concorde from service was in this respect a symptomatic event: we had attained the maximal speed and at least for economic reasons we will not exceed it for a long time. On our globe that we call minuscule, space is expanding and our means of transportation are re-creating the distance that they were supposed to abolish. But we never kill one passion without substituting another for it. Our shimmering machines have been replaced by our mobile phones, computers that allow us to be everywhere without leaving home and connected with everyone with being with anyone. A miracle of the miniaturized world: instead of energy-gulping monsters, we have 'nomadic objects' with flat screens and multiple functions, a whole universe in a tool that weighs a few hundred grams and that we will soon be able to build into our bodies. Freedom united with ubiquity.

2

Have the Courage to be Afraid

Don't be scared to be afraid, have the courage to be afraid. And have the courage to scare others. Communicate to your neighbours a fear at least as great as your own.

Günther Anders, *La Menace nucléaire*, 1960

A lesser disaster now will avoid a greater one in the future.

Theodore Kaczynski (a.k.a. 'The Unabomber'),
The Road to Revolution, 2008

In Austria, at the end of the nineteenth century, a physician was called to the bedside of a young woman who was giving birth in an inn. Her husband, a drunken brute, had just been appointed as a customs official in the neighbouring town. She gave birth to a frail, puny child, a boy whom she named Adolfus. She had already lost three babies shortly after birth and was afraid that this one would die as well. On looking at the stunted infant, the father was frightened as well. The doctor ordered him to show a little tenderness toward his wife and to kiss her. She wept, asking those present to witness her prayers that her baby would not die. On leaving, the doctor put his hand on the husband's shoulder. 'You must forget the others, Herr Hitler. Give this one a chance.' This extraordinary story told by Roald Dahl[1] raises an important problem: can evil be averted by acting at its source, can the future be predicted with such accuracy that one can prevent it from coming?

Maximal indictment

The rhetoric of fear is denounced by everyone, in every camp, but only the better to substitute another for it. Each individual sees it in accord with his or her ideological assumptions. Catholics proclaim, through the voice of John Paul II, 'Be not afraid', but they denounce the absence of God in the contemporary world and moral relativism, the source of dreadful aberrations. The right wing ridicules the absurd fear of the market and free enterprise, but emphasizes urban insecurity and the decay of morals. The left wing follows suit, mocking the blackmail based on terrorism and delinquency – in its view, stories about crime are mere diversions – but underlines the dangers of globalization and global warming. All our fears are constructed; in a certain way, we always choose the misfortune against which we want to protect ourselves. Tell me what I have to fear so that I can get my bearings in life. People rightly laughed at the campaign mounted in 2009 against the A (H1N1) 'swine flu' virus, which turned out to be less virulent than had been thought, and suspected the World Health Organization of being influenced by pharmaceutical laboratories that wanted to dispose of their vaccines. Had this form of flu killed people, public opinion would have accused public officials of negligence and a lack of preparation.

Fear has the power to mobilize people, to get them to overcome their divisions by proposing an object of collective repulsion, designating a scapegoat that binds them together and leads them to put their fates in the hands of a third party. That was Hobbes's project in his *Leviathan* (1651): to generate from human impotence a new political order, to offer individuals the protection of the state in exchange for the surrender of their personal liberty. Man being a wolf to his fellow men – *Homo homini lupus* – he achieves tranquillity by delegating his powers to a sovereign who safeguards them for him. The fear of dying becomes a reasonable passion when it halts the war of all against all by subjecting citizens to the will of a single individual. Today, as in Hobbes's time, anxiety has been elevated to the status of a political virtue, whereas joy is seen as a sign of unawareness. Formerly, one had to tame one's fears; now, for those who 'feel the planet's pain' (Nicolas Hulot), they have to be cultivated. Professors of dread strive to tell you the difference between legitimate and puerile apprehensions. A philosopher (Paul Virilio) has even proposed to create a 'university of disaster'[2] that would study, among other things, the understanding of limits 'in the sense that the Earth is too small and the world is foreclosed'. It is Hans Jonas who has made the 'heuristics of fear' a tool of knowledge and foresight, a way of sparing future generations the dangers inherent in technology.[3] Fear and trembling have become indispensable, because we cannot predict our instruments' destructive potential. But the temptation is great to abuse this feeling and to substitute the dictatorship of fear for the government of reason. Jonas himself, distrusting democracy, advocated a 'well-intentioned, well-informed tyranny' of enlightened people capable of taking into account the stakes involved in ecology.[4]

In the United States, after September 11 we saw the Bush administration using the war on terrorism to justify all kinds of distortions of the legal system: silencing opponents, arbitrarily arresting suspects, and forming alliances with treacherous or corrupt regimes in order to defeat Al-Qaeda. Then looms the danger of a gradual dismantling of the rule of law that was manifested by the adoption of the Patriot Act (October 2001), which gave the police and intelligence services exorbitant powers to violate individual privacy, to wiretap, and to subvert institutions.[5] We may wonder whether Al-Qaeda, partly defeated militarily, didn't win on at least one point: it undermined the whole edifice of rights and freedoms characteristic of parliamentary systems by forcing them to protect themselves, to betray themselves. The same security procedures that are supposed to protect us against terrorist attack make each of us a potential suspect. Victims and tormentors are treated without distinction. We are searched and monitored in order to be reassured. Thus there is a danger of destroying democracy in order to save it, of multiplying criminal categories, of putting a whole country under police surveillance. The culture of fear has always been the favourite instrument of dictatorships: democracies can make use of it only to a limited extent without destroying themselves. To espouse the logic of one's enemies the better to defeat them is to reproduce them here in order to destroy them there.

Apocalyptic religion uses the same procedures: it frightens, it literally creates the fear from which it seeks to protect us. The first axiom is: we are all responsible for the world's misfortunes, whether we want to be or not:

> Until recently, the effects of ordinary people's actions concerned almost exclusively those close to them. This is no longer the case for the consumer who contributes, indirectly [. . .] to the effects of distance [. . .]. Many peasants in the Nile delta or the Gulf of Bengal are already forced to abandon lands that have been devoted for centuries to agriculture because they have become too saline as a result of the pressure of a rise in sea level attributable to climate change.[6]

By its simple mechanism our everyday life causes terrible damage. Selfish concern about one's own comfort can be just as lethal as premeditated murder. Eating, lodging, and travelling make us potential assassins whose most innocuous acts have incalculable repercussions. Jean-Pierre Dupuy, a brilliant disciple of René Girard and Ivan Illich, tells us that '[t]he distinction between killing by an intentional individual act and killing because one cares only about one's own welfare as a citizen of a rich country, whereas others are dying of hunger – that distinction is less and less tenable.'[7]

A whole civilization irrevocably condemns itself and seeks to invert the order of the centuries, to undo, like Penelope, the tapestry that it has patiently woven. The danger comes from us, the opulent Westerners whose mode of production, if it were extended to everyone, would lay waste to the earth. We are enemies to the human race but also to ourselves, because we are digging our own graves and those of our children.

'The Western standard of living is not moral.'[8] We are innocents with bloody hands, or rather people who are guilty without malice – a little, making due allowances, like the pilots who dropped atom bombs on Hiroshima and Nagasaki: they were not motivated by any animosity against the people they were going to annihilate.[9] But our passivity barely conceals an absolute consent.

'[T]he daily exercise of our powers, which makes the routine of modern civilization possible and which we all depend on, becomes an ethical problem' (Hans Jonas).[10] We have to expiate sins that we have not wanted to commit, on the condition that we become aware of them. In the words of Joseph de Maistre, a French theorist of the Counter-Revolution and the defender of a vengeful theodicy: 'There is no righteous man on Earth.'[11]

Here the trick is to reverse the burden of proof. Instead of requiring, for instance, that climatologists prove the reality of global warming, people ask them to prove that the cataclysm will not occur. The scepticism that up to that point was seen as an index of wisdom has become a symptom of blindness. How can we fail to recall here the sophism used by President Bush in March 2003, on the eve of the second Gulf War? Asked by journalists if it was a proven fact that Saddam Hussein had weapons of mass destruction, he gave this answer worthy of the best sophists: 'Absence of proof is not proof of absence.' Jean-Pierre Dupuy goes him one better, on a smaller scale: in the domain of technological or commercial innovation, the apparent innocuousness of a product just means that its toxicity has not yet been proven. 'Thus it is up to the innovator to prove that his product is not harmful, and the absence of proofs that it is does not suffice to prove it.'[12]

If an object's utility or harmfulness can be proven solely by using it, then the only way to be safe is never to use it, to sterilize all innovation. The possibility of danger is thus transformed into a certainty. In the case of Iraq, the suspicion that terrible events might occur if the Western powers did not intervene immediately dismissed doubts as frivolous. Fear gives its objects a greater weight than reality: think of drowning people who in their terror drag their rescuers down with them or people who jump off precipices for fear that they will fall. 'Fear is absurd,' Kant said long ago, 'it fears the very thing from which it expects help.'

Trained to panic

The phenomenon of self-fulfilling prophecies: for instance, the media are amazed to discover among the younger generation the obsession with global warming that they are constantly instilling in it. As in an echo chamber, polls reflect an opinion formatted by the media. Fear is injected by the repetition of the same themes, and it becomes a narcotic we can no longer do without. To wake others up, people boldly go to extremes. For instance, the *reductio ad Hitlerum*, as when Michel Rocard compared our passivity with regard to rising temperatures to 'a crime against humanity', no less![13] Thus the vocabulary of the Shoah is annexed to meteorological phenomena. Noël Mamère, a Green Party delegate in the French National Assembly, went so far as to call the scientist and Socialist politician Claude Allègre a 'climate denier', an allusion to deniers of the Jewish and Armenian genocides. Rajendra Pachauri, an economist who is chairman of the Group of Intergovernmental Experts on Climate (GIEC), has himself compared the Danish statistician Bjorn Lomborg, an eco-sceptic, to Adolf Hitler. In 2007, an American climatologist who works for NASA, James Hansen, accused oil companies that seek to minimize the impact of climate change of a 'crime against humanity and nature', and identified trains carrying American coal to the trains that carried victims to death camps during World War II! Ellen Goodman, an editorial writer for the *Boston Globe*, wrote on 9 February 2007 that 'global warming deniers are on a par with Holocaust deniers'.

The palm goes to the president of Bolivia, Evo Morales, who exclaimed in a vast synthesis delivered in December 2010 at the Caracas conference: 'If we junk the Kyoto protocol, we will be responsible for an economicide, an ecocide, a genocide, because it is an attack on humanity as a whole.' Better yet: the conditional is done away with and people already speak the language of the future in the present, so that any chance of a possible recovery is disqualified.

Like the swimmers in Thailand who saw only at the last moment the gigantic wave breaking over them, we seem not to perceive the hundreds of millions of unfortunates who, driven out of their homes by drought, rising sea levels, hurricanes or storms, will soon seek asylum with us to flee not only oppressive regimes but also territories that we will have devastated through our carelessness without even knowing them [. . .]. Today, political action must no longer be conceived from the point of view of a revolution to be carried out but from that of the catastrophe to be averted, if there is still time to do so.[14]

And again Al Gore:

Humanity is sitting on a ticking time bomb. If the vast majority of the world's scientists are right, we have just ten years to avert a major catastrophe that could send our entire planet into a tail-spin of epic destruction involving extreme weather, floods, droughts, epidemics and killer heat waves beyond anything we have ever experienced.[15]

Gore asserts that we will be primarily responsible for this catastrophe of an unprecedented magnitude, and that we alone can still avoid it.

An unchanging rhetorical figure, well known to preachers and propagandists, recurs in the cataclysmic discourse: that of retroactive correction. It proceeds by accumulating new horrors that it ends up tempering with a thin ray of hope. It begins by breaking down all resistance before offering dazed audiences a way out: although as a good American Al Gore refuses to yield to defeatism, the enormity of the message he conveys can only encourage distress. All catastrophist discourses suffer from a twofold contradiction: if the situation is as serious as they claim, why fight against it? Why not sit back and await the deluge? But the proposed solutions are ludicrous in view of the perils. As a rule, information has value only if it leads to concrete action: telling us, for example, that 'the oceans are on the brink of a biological crisis unprecedented in 55 million years',[16] or that marine ecosystems will all collapse between now and 2050, is simply bewildering. This news prohibits any reaction other than distress and passivity. To then offer 'recommendations' is to contradict the gravity of the message. Consider the ways of reducing our CO_2 emissions that the ex-vice president, like most ecologists, proposes: replacing our light bulbs by low-consumption models, checking our tyre pressure, recycling waste, rejecting excessive packaging, turning down thermostats, planting a tree, turning off electrical devices (DVD readers, stereos, computers). All this for that! *The enormity of the diagnosis, the absurd inadequacy of the remedies.* Like good boy scouts, the Greens offer us endless home economics advice worthy of our grand-mothers. Since we have been dispossessed of any power with respect to the planet, we're going to convert this impotence into little propitiatory gestures, climbing stairs instead of taking the elevator, becoming vegetarians, riding bicycles – anything that gives us the illusion of acting. Let's be clear: a cosmic calamity is not going to be averted by eating vegetables and sorting our rubbish.

On the one hand, we are told that because of technology's power we can no longer predict the fallout from our acts; on the other hand, we are exhorted to 'give up driving big cars, change a diet that includes too much meat, cut back on [our] air travel', in short, 'consume fewer material goods'.[17] How can we be sure that these restrictions will have a positive effect, since we cannot know the consequences of our most ordinary acts? This is the aporia of Green neo-asceticism: it gives to every-day behaviours an enormous importance that invalidates its appeal for humility. An overestimation of the power of the human being, whom Descartes described as 'the master and possessor of nature' and is now called 'the destroyer and repairer of the cosmos'! So we can heal our good old Earth simply by becoming pedestrians? What boastfulness! On this level at least, those who demand a general slow-down of human activities and a return to past centuries are being logical. Catastrophism terrorizes us first in order to calm us later on by proposing little ritual gestures worthy of a post-technological animism.

Before becoming an instrument of political manipulation, fear is a singular aesthetic motor. Human genius has been able to make this base feeling a great source of pleasure. It is important to be made aware in early childhood of the reality of evil, to listen to stories of kidnappings, torture, and dungeons in order to learn how powerless individuals can escape their tormentors. The weak against the strong, the innocent against the wicked, that is what all these stories are about. Fiction keeps us at a distance from the horror and we emerge from it purged and regenerated. As Bruno Bettelheim explains concerning fairy tales, these stories about witches, ogres, and poisoned apples correspond to children's anxieties and tell them about the trials to come, while offering the elegant solution that will lead them toward maturity.[18] This solution is illustrated by Bettelheim's famous analysis of the story of the Three Little Pigs who want to escape the Big Bad Wolf. The first little pig builds a house of straw that the wolf destroys with a simple puff of breath. The second builds a house of wood that the wolf knocks down with a blow of his paw. The third little pig has built a house of bricks. The wolf tries and tries to destroy the house, but cannot. When he tries to go down the chimney, the pigs put a boiling cauldron on the hearth that scalds the wolf. The moral of the story, according to Bettelheim, is that the first two pigs acted in accord with the pleasure principle, that is, with the least effort possible, while the third submitted to the reality principle and saved his skin. He had to show courage and rationality in order to defeat his pursuer. Children who listen to this story acquire the ability to find their way in life and to resolve difficult problems.

The same can be said about two minor genres, horror and catastrophe films, which also have a cathartic aim: to purge us of our fears by focusing our attention on a specific peril. To be scared for hours on end while watching mobs of zombies, a tower on fire, or an aeroplane crash is to free oneself temporarily from one's malaise by contemplating a limited danger. Our vague fear is replaced by a definite one. Anxiety, having no object because it is the anxiety of existing, has to be played out in fictions that embody it. People who are terrified no longer feel afraid, being completely absorbed by their terror. For an hour or two, in darkened spaces, the show blurs our points of reference, fills the real with its phantasmagorias, calms minds that are prey to demons. That is the whole paradox of the fear that reassures us, purges us of our uneasiness. Gothic and fantastic stories, which were so admired in past centuries, provided the twofold pleasure of abomination and reward.[19]

In the United States the function of Halloween is also to set fixed dates for fear in the pagan form of children disguised as ghosts and skeletons running through the streets and knocking on doors to demand candy.

In the idyllic setting of a mountain lake, a picnic in the countryside, or a prosperous small town, evil strikes with the suddenness of a lightning bolt and all hell breaks loose. Tenderly embracing couples and happy, laughing families are massacred, dismembered with chainsaws, hung on meat hooks by a psychopath or a clan of degenerates. Everything happens in a day or two in a series of visual shocks and violent effects. The worst is always still to come, and when we think we've touched bottom, a new abomination surges up that makes our flesh creep. We gradually lose our footing as the story proceeds through a series of uppercuts that knock us out. Fear is an infection of space and time, the progressive corruption of the everyday by a gangrene that eats away at it. The great film directors excel at this construction of the uneasiness that slowly corrodes space and time. The most ordinary aspects of life, sleeping, eating, taking a shower – remember the fundamental scene in *Psycho*, with its butcher's knife and torn shower curtain – are pregnant with unimagined danger. In this sense, paranoia, a dangerous political passion, is a marvellous fictional motor: it awakens powers hidden in everyday life, intensifies routine by raising it to the level of a conspiracy. The exception becomes the norm. It puts us in a universe where we are warned and called upon to choose between life and death. We have to act immediately, on pain of death. Apocalyptic discourse is never anything but a transposition into the political sphere of the rules of horror movies. That is why the United States, obsessed by imaginary conspiracies despite its flaunted optimism, has also made all the classic horror films and remains one of the world's great narrative laboratories in this domain.

Film is a sifting system that is supposed to affect us as it protects. Kant and Edmund Burke defined the sublime as a horrifying spectacle that we enjoy because we are far away from it: a mixture of terror and elevation, it confronts us with a vision that goes beyond us and transports us. It was in the seventeenth century that mountains, and especially the Alps, ceased to be hideous protuberances and started to become aesthetic spectacles worthy of attention.[20] Yesterday's monster may become today's marvel. The whole task of cinematic form will thus consist in making a choice. Terror is delicious when it moves us without affecting us directly. We emerge from a good film relieved if it has been able to give consistency to our concern, dissipate our mental disturbances. Distance permits catharsis. Our hair stands on end, and after an emergency landing or a group massacre, we follow, panting with anticipation, the epic adventures of the survivors. What would I have done in such circumstances?

In film and in novels, how many unfortunates expire before our eyes, increasing our joy at not being the one who is dying. The eighteenth-century English gentleman, a historian tells us, delighted in public executions, seeing in them an opportunity to experience strong feelings.[21] The appetite for police procedurals and thrillers in democratic societies is inversely proportional to our propensity to commit criminal acts. The more a people civilizes and restrains its murderous impulses, the more it takes pleasure in atrocious stories. In the same way, the disaster film, with its disembowelled cities and flattened skyscrapers, is a levelling utopia in which rich and poor are eliminated without distinction, as well as a lesson in modesty, like the 'vanities' of the *Ancien Régime*, those grinning skulls that reminded the frivolous classes of the fleeting nature of existence. The most astonishing edifices, the vastest empires are doomed to be destroyed. Woe to anyone who forgets it!

We have to be safe to appreciate the spectacle of nature in an uproar, a raging storm or tornado that reminds us of our insignificance. The cinema allows us to experience the thrill of danger without actually being in danger. Snug in our seats, we enjoy the horror without the consequences that would result were we immersed in it (some facetious managers of cinemas specializing in fantastic films have gone so far as to install mechanical hands that touched spectators' shoulders or necks at the crucial moment). We come close to the worst without risking more than the price of a ticket. Obviously, everything changes when we are directly confronted with a dangerous situation. As we know, there are hurricane buffs who enjoy being at the very eye of the storm where everything is calm while the storm rages all around them. Anyone who has done a bit of mountain or rock climbing knows how much fear increases the emotional yield of an ascension. To cope with sheer cliffs, walls of ice, and treacherous ridges is to vanquish what overwhelms us. To know the 'fizzing, nauseating, faintly erotic feeling of real terror', to adopt the terms of the British alpinist Robert Macfarlane, to endure vertigo, pain, and frostbite, is to carry out a transmutation of oneself. Without the ultimate risk, without the fear of dying buried or crushed under an avalanche, there is no pleasure. '[W]e never feel so alive as when we have nearly died.'[22]

An ambiguous moral: there is pleasure to be taken in seeing fictional characters die, but it is a relief to see their ability to find a way out of the worst situations. The horror film, like the disaster film, is a borderline genre: not only does it take place at the intersection of the everyday world and the supernatural world, but it pushes ordinary people to their limits, makes them powerless victims or heroes in spite of themselves. As in the film *The Road*,[23] an adaptation of a novel by Cormac McCarthy, in which a father and his son flee toward the ocean through an America that has been ravaged by a nuclear winter and in which gangs of cannibals are lying in wait. Every minute is a door through which death can strike, every wanderer they meet is a potential murderer. These ordinary people grappling with an exceptional situation have to draw on resources of their own that are themselves exceptional. To narrate an accident or an aggression that has befallen us is to narrate a miracle, that of our survival. We have to free ourselves from the spell by means of the words of peril overcome.

The return of the grim reaper

It is not surprising that the apogee of the horror film is contemporary with the emergence of ecology some thirty years ago. Both reflect the obsession with violent death in a world that had masked it since the war. Anyone can be a victim, as in the case of mass murders or natural cataclysms. The action is sometimes set in a place where an initial crime has been committed but not avenged; the punishment then falls on the distant descendants of the murderer or on innocent hikers guilty of being in the wrong place at the wrong time, just as our children will pay for our terrible negligence regarding technology. Zombie films tell us in particular that the dead must always be killed a second time to ensure their definitive burial. They also suggest that the living are already dead without knowing it, whereas the dead are far more alive than they are. Philippe Ariès reminded us that in ancient Rome and after, one of the goals of funerary cults 'was to prevent the dead from coming back to disturb the living'.[24] Their resentment and anger at having died before others had to be appeased. For that reason, most cemeteries were located outside cities, a custom that changed with the beginning of Christianity, when the dead were brought back into the cities, and the bones of the holy martyrs in particular were placed near churches. In Renaissance Europe, a macabre art with erotic connotations developed, with love scenes in tombs depicting corpses that had retained their genitals, like the Four Horsemen of the Apocalypse in Dürer's famous painting, and were capable of raping young mortals: people took pleasure in seeing flayed bodies lying on dissecting tables during anatomy lessons. In the eighteenth century, dissection became an art for amateurs who collected cadavers with veins and muscles exposed. The theme of the dead who produced strange sounds, devoured their shrouds, and came to sow terror in the countrysides, sometimes spreading epidemics of plague, appeared as early as the sixteenth century. Just as since 1945 death has become the supreme form of pornography in the West – sex is no longer hidden, it is on stage, displayed in the media, on billboards – the theme of the living dead rising from the earth to bury us has reappeared in popular culture, especially since George Romero's cult film.[25] Driven out of discourse, euphemized, confined in hospital rooms, death is making a strong comeback as a symptom in the minor genres and in catastrophism.

A strange mix-up: seen with respect to a nuclear holocaust, the philosopher Günther Anders tells us, we are 'all, without exception and without distinction, dead people on reprieve and we constitute [. . .] one great mass of victims'.[26] In horror films, the dead all have a burst of life that leads them to rise to the surface, hideous and stumbling, in order to devour us. The simple fact of coming after 80 billion other humans makes us criminals rising out of heaps of corpses. A change in scale: today, with nuclear weapons, we have to add to the mortality of the individual person that of the species as such. Nuclear weapons embody on the collective level the fate allotted to each of us: the certainty of possible annihilation at any moment. The precariousness of life characteristic of the Middle Ages is extended to the whole world. We live longer but the human race as such can be annihilated in an instant.

What are the living dead? Absent-minded beings who got their dates mixed up and came back too early, parodying the promised resurrection at the end of time: they have to be killed once again so that they can rest in peace. Just as we are born at least twice, first to life and then as ourselves, we always die twice, the first time when our vital functions stop, the second when the completion of mourning places us in the great series of those who have passed away. We never die precisely on the day of our deaths: either before or afterward. It takes a certain amount of time for those close to us to realize that we are no longer there. For example, there is nothing sadder for artists than to survive their reputations, so that everyone thinks they died years before. In the first zombie films, the stumbling, grotesque gait of the revenants gave you the illusion that you could escape them. The directors' sole innovation – which may reflect an increase in fear – is to have given them more speed.

These swifter corpses, who are sometimes awakened by a virus and in whom a friend, father, neighbour, or daughter might be recognized, their flesh already eaten away by vermin, can run as fast as we can. They are indefatigable stiffs who are starving and eat everything, even animals, and contaminate you with their first bite. Death catches up with us everywhere, it patiently awaits its chance, because we carry it within us, in the air we breathe, in the tissues that compose us, in the beating of our hearts.

The limits of the horror show

During the Cold War, strategists like Herman Kahn worked out nuclear war scenarios in order 'to think the unthinkable' and prepare for a possible conflict.[27] Today, the Pentagon uses experts in special effects to spare soldiers on the battlefield, and also uses writers whose job is to describe possible accidents. Before September 11, several Hollywood productions had imagined similar attacks. A catastrophe is a scenario that has succeeded. We draw on our cinematographic memory to recognize an event that is new but which we have nonetheless already seen. The future may be written somewhere in a book we haven't read or in a B-movie we watched absent-mindedly and that will someday be exhumed, after a tragedy. The simulation of the worst-case scenario by those responsible for nuclear, civil, and industrial security is a way of recognizing risks in order to neutralize them. We must always have an accident in view. When the same kind of simulation is carried out by catastrophists, its only goal is to paralyse us. We will not escape; the future will destroy us!

Cataclysmic ecology reflects the triumph of guilt: children must pay for the errors of their elders – progress, development, consumerism. It inaugurates a universe

saturated with crimes, mourning, sorrow: the profana-
tion of nature must be sanctioned by an implacable
punishment. But like any narrative, it is subject to a
requirement of balance that provides its persuasive
force. Three genres degenerate when they forget the
constraints of moderation: below a certain level of ignominy, the horror film descends into mere gore,[28] the
police drama sinks into the ridiculous when it piles up
murders and mutilations, and the X-rated film becomes
boring when it multiplies genital or gynaecological
acrobatics. The images go too far and lose their power
of transgression. Apathy is born from excess: from
blood, violence, and mechanical copulation. Emotion
dies away, killed by immoderation. Where we are supposed to be tremble, we yawn or laugh: outrage that
has become routine overcomes the most terrifying
images. Political discourse also runs out of steam when
it indulges in exaggeration. Sometimes a bit of involuntary humour slips in amid the most sensational remarks:
'When the oceans have warmed up, we will have no
way of cooling them down again.'[29] A marvellous observation – reminiscent of Flaubert's *Bouvard and Pecu-
chet* – that works both ways. One feels like responding:
'Sure we will – just put ice cubes in them!' If gloomy
prophesying too often fails to convince, that is because
it defuses its predictions by its tendency to go to
extremes.

The matrix of the whole environmentalist discourse
is the story of the Fall in Genesis: in the beginning there
was the earthly paradise, but humans ate of the fruit of
the tree of knowledge, and God drove them out. At the
same time that Europe denies its Christian roots, it
manifests them in its slightest references: our thinking
takes place more than ever in light of the Bible, whose
lexicon and structure continue to be at work in our
everyday life. We all date the damnation in our own
ways. For Rousseau, our misfortune began with the

invention of metallurgy and agriculture, that is, with private property, and we soon saw 'slavery and wretchedness sprouting and growing along with the harvests'.[30] For others, damnation is the modern world (René Guénon): 'a monstrosity [. . .] a civilization built on something negative, on what might be called an absence of principles';[31] for others still, it is the Enlightenment, the industrial revolution, mechanization, techno-scientism,[32] and the manipulation of the atom and DNA, 'two boundaries that man ought not to have crossed' (Ewing Chargas). Ultimately, the catastrophe has always already taken place; it began as soon as primitive humans invented the first tools and moved away from Being. In reality, humanity as a whole is only a history of collapse ever since the expulsion from Eden. Today, humans find themselves in the Hell of development, from which they have to escape if they are not to destroy their planet. Forests cut down, mountains disembowelled, animals decimated, oceans polluted, unliveable megalopolises: our period is completely bankrupt; there is no doubt as to its atrociousness. Doing nothing is tantamount to complicity or even crime. We have to wake up before it's too late, because 'we can still transform the threat into a desirable and credible promise'.[33] But this excessive excitement frightens us without rousing us to action. The exhibition of the horrible, the litany of statistics repeated over and over, ends up producing a kind of tolerance. The risk inherent in a certain type of rhetoric is that it will degenerate into a jeremiad without substance. The goal is to alarm us, but we are merely disarmed.

There is a certain irony in the fact that the most rabid propagators of cowardice deplore our apathy, whereas that is exactly what they seek to produce:

On pain of heading for catastrophe, protecting the environment is an imperative that can no longer be eluded. And yet in this domain an astonishing

wait-and-see policy prevails. Crucial questions receive
no more than polite attention; reforms that involve the
future of humanity are put off [. . .]. That is the paradox
in which we find ourselves today: scientists' warnings
regarding the danger and the urgency of the situation
leave us cold.[34]

The fact is that this flood of bad news seeks only to
demoralize us and bring us to heel, like children, with
a scolding solicitude. The point is to overwhelm us, to
deprive us of any capacity for action. Giving fear the
status of a rational guide to action assumes that the
danger is perceptible and the gain evident: that alone
distinguishes legitimate warning from frenzied alarmism. The former arises from an immediate danger
that we can still avert through collective or individual
action. Fighting a laboratory that is keeping on the
market a dangerous drug or a chemical compound that
is poisoning a whole region is not the same thing as
imagining that one is responsible for humanity's destiny
centuries from now. In one case, it is up to us to prevent
a misfortune; in the other we are subject to incommen-
surable obligations. A democracy is all the more alive
for having 'sacrificial sentinels', individuals, associations, great consciences that uncover the shameful
secrets and dirty work of the powerful and denounce
scandals. The news today is full of stories in which
researchers and journalists have risked their reputations
and even their lives with an obstinacy that demands our
admiration.

But how can we mobilize to cope with a virtual risk
when the length of time involved extends to centuries
or even millennia? In January 2011, Canadian computer
scientists using simulations predicted that the Earth,
through the simple effect of inertia, would take more
than a thousand years to get rid of the CO_2 emissions
produced during the twentieth century! Let's assume
that's right. Then what? Such projections are beyond

any empirical test: who will be there a thousand years from now to say whether they are right? These are hypotheses that are intellectually exciting but that invalidate any mobilization. The credibility of a disaster can be based only on tangible elements. If we must, as Hans Jonas demands, reverse the Cartesian postulate and doubt everything except the worst, which thereby becomes indubitable,[35] then we have to abandon our immediate concerns in the name of the plague that is threatening us. In order to escape the uncertainty of history, the certainty of chaos is decreed; this allows us to settle back into the cushy sweetness of the execrable. In order to avert the horror, we have to act as if it were inevitable![36] But the *as if* has become more real than the real, which is reduced to the status of a phantom in comparison to the imminence of the reverses that are piling up. Catastrophe is the most reasonable hypothesis, and it is to our advantage to believe in it in order to avoid the infinite cost that would have to be paid if it turned out to be correct.

Yes, to be sure. But to validate the gloomiest axioms so long as they have not been disproven, as the principle of precaution calls upon us to do, is to forget that history also surprises us with its good sides; it is to neglect 'the fecundity of the unexpected' (Proudhon). In the sequence of causes and effects, something new and better can appear. Ten years ago, who could have foreseen the amazing boom in India, China, and Brazil, which has raised hundreds of millions of people out of poverty (but for die-hard ecologists, this miracle is a calamity)? Who would have suspected the Arab uprisings in all their complexity, and the overthrow of tyrants? The classic detective novel tells the story of a crime that disturbs the social order and has to be solved in order to restore the peace. The crime novel describes a world of continuous disorder in which murder and corruption never cease and form the stuff of everyday existence. In the same way, the classical age of stability disturbed by an accident is succeeded by the age of permanent disturbance: we are entering into an age of 'mega-risks' (Patrick Lagadec) that can bring all economic and social systems to a halt because they are interdependent. Human genius consists in surviving plagues, in drawing from them lessons that enable us not to reproduce them. We recall the famous remark made by Adorno in 1949, to which he returned later on: 'There can be no poetry after Auschwitz.' There is no catastrophe so terrible that societies cannot survive it, bruised but alive. Where gloomy people see a guilty carelessness, we should discern on the contrary a formidable resistance. Life goes on: that platitude is the answer to all the prophets of doom. Healing may be slow, but in the end it happens. Life went on in Europe after 1945 – a relatively large Jewish community was re-established in Germany and even in Poland – and it will continue in Japan after Fukushima, even if the survivors have to avoid the criminal negligence that led to the disaster. Let us not underestimate the capacity for resistance and solidarity among peoples who seem to be benumbed by well-being. When the storm strikes, when the flood comes, an evil genius may lead the faint-hearted to save their own skins, but a good genius arouses courage, mutual aid, and heroism in others. Catastrophe reveals the worst and the best in human beings.

Fear can be thought but it does not think. It attaches the subject to the object of its dread the way a fly sticks to flypaper. It immobilizes and then produces a mental and physical somnolence that can be fatal. It can awaken us but it can also paralyse us, and even precipitate the misfortune that it was supposed to protect us against. Thus there are two kinds of fear: a salutary one that mobilizes us, and a deleterious one that weakens us. Terror is the surest path to servitude.

A Brief Contemporary Lexicon

Every age produces its linguistic pathologies and unites people around a few mantras that they repeat to reassure themselves. If reality cannot be changed, it can be redescribed to make it more attractive.

ETHICAL. This old-fashioned adjective, more chic than moral, surrounds each term with an aroma of saintliness. It lifts any hint of suspicion from all sorts of activities. We can speak of ethical marketing, ethical tourism, and an ethical diet, as well as ethical ballpoint pens.

ETHNIC. Opposed to 'majority', 'ethnic' combines the moral force of a minority, which is always oppressed, with the profundity of authenticity. Whatever is ethnic is delicious and colourful, while what is not is tasteless and pale.

EQUITABLE. Equitable commerce, or 'fair trade' as it is often called in English, consists in assuring a fair income for producers in developing countries so that they can continue to work under good conditions, even though this entails extra costs. This label gives products such as coffee, textiles, and craft objects a slightly paternalistic touch of legitimacy. When a product is simultaneously ethnic, ethical, and equitable, it accumulates the maximum of meaning and justice. Adding 'eco' ('ecological' has won out over 'economical') and 'bio' to any word is enough to sanctify it. What is sought, through the proliferation of abbreviations, is neither more nor less than absolution. The nomenclature has a purifying aim.

CITIZENS. By what operation has 'citizens''
become an adjective to be used in every context?
The loss of a civic sense and civility goes along
with the inflation of the epithet 'citizens'', which
is expected to provide a sound foundation for a
debate, an initiative, a concert, a market.

SUSTAINABLE. Everything now has to be sustainable, development as well as mobility, the future
as well as love. For the sake of preservation at any
cost, people would like to do away with the ephemeral, the 'poignant grandeur' (Péguy) of the perish-
able. Isn't the problem with progress, with waste,
with plastic bags, precisely that they are durable,
that they stubbornly cling to existence? Hasn't an
American author demonstrated that in the event of
humanity's disappearance, the remains of our cities
and factories would continue to exist for at least
500 years, despite the erosion and deterioration of
their materials?[37] If everything started being
durable, life would quickly turn into a nightmare.
We would lose the tremendous charm of that
which passes and never returns, and of which
nature itself, with its cycle of seasons, provides a
fine example. We would lose what Buddhism nicely
calls the impermanence of things.

ANOTHER WORLD IS POSSIBLE. Why has this
slogan aged so badly? It is part of the same order
of expression as Rimbaud's famous remark that
'Real life is elsewhere', a way of disqualifying our
world, which is guilty of being only what it is. To
choose another life as one's ideal is to denigrate
this one instead of fulfilling it in all its dimensions.
We can fight for a better world, but why does it
have to be 'other'? Then we fall back into the error
religious systems are reproached for committing:

the disease of renunciation. Tomorrow will be different, and that allows us to put up with today: an old ascetic technique. The solution is merely verbal: a complex reality is clothed in a new semantic garb.

3

Blackmailing Future Generations

Everything is foreseen except, naturally, what is going to happen.
René Ladreit de Lacharrière (1833–1903)

The best way to predict the future is to invent it.
Dominique Nora, *Les Pionniers de l'or vert*, 2009

In 1954, Leon Festinger, a young psychologist who later formulated the theory of 'cognitive dissonance', infiltrated, along with two of his colleagues, a millenarian sect in Illinois that had predicted a flood that would end the world on 12 December of that year.[1] The leader of the group, Dorothy Martin (called 'Marian Keech' in Festinger's book), claimed to have received by automatic writing messages from superior beings from a planet named Clarion. The disciples were feverishly preparing for the end of the world, certain that they would be rescued by an armada of flying saucers. They were given a passport for embarkation (in fact it was a simple notebook) and asked to dispose of any metallic objects – one of them even had to cut open his fly in order to be admitted on board. They learned the password by heart – 'I left my hat at home' – and were assigned seat numbers in the spaceship.[2] For four days and nights, they waited in the bitter cold for their saviours' arrival, on the lookout for a blaze in the sky, a celestial glow. Multiple counter-orders issued by a 'creator' helped them wait patiently and allowed them to retain their convictions. They had all quit their jobs, hocked their possessions, and said goodbye to their families. But on the morning of 24 December, they had to accept the obvious: the flood wasn't going to happen, and America was preparing to celebrate Christmas. The 'elect' had to endure their friends' and families' mockery and the gibes of the press. Disappointment reached its peak and the first defections began.

Then a miracle occurred: the factual refutation turned into a confirmation of belief. A new message from the 'superior beings' postponed the punishment's date: at the last minute, God, in his immense benevolence, decided to spare His children. He accorded them an additional period to redeem themselves. The faithful began preaching again; proselytizing resumed on an even greater scale. They engaged in multiple conversations, thought they saw spacemen everywhere who had come to encourage them, looked for signs on television screens, and recorded telephone calls in the hope that they might contain a whisper, a subliminal message that would tell them what to do. The error in the prediction was transformed into a confirmation of its veracity. What should have abolished faith reinvigorated it. Finally the sect dissolved because it lacked apostles eloquent enough to recruit new followers. Isn't it the peculiarity of a certain kind of messianism that it resists any counter-evidence, remaining impermeable to refutations because it has always known what had to occur? 'Convictions are more dangerous enemies of truth than lies' (Nietzsche, *Human, All Too Human*).

The voluptuous pleasure of the state
of emergency

Why do we take such pleasure, in the West, in predicting our own disappearance? In situations of all-out war, foreseeing the worst is a proof of lucidity: 'The optimists died in the gas chambers; the pessimists have pools in Beverly Hills,' Billy Wilder remarked wittily in 1945. There can be a desperate optimism and an active pessimism, a source of energy. But defeatism is also the second home of privileged peoples, the contented sigh of big cats purring in comfort. Thanks to the media, we move in a cacophonous space that mixes an earthquake in Japan with rumination on our little lives. A tragedy that strikes far away transforms the platitude of our everyday lives into a high-risk adventure: we are living on the edge of the abyss! Lucretius already showed us the wise man seated on a cliff by the sea, contemplating the madmen – sailors and ship captains – drowning in the turbulent waves. Television brings the horror into our homes, at dinnertime, making us present at the event as if it had happened near us. But it does not necessarily make us feel that the other's misfortune is our own; instead, it confirms our belief in the fragility of our well-being. The involuntary humour of apocalyptic discourse resides in its tendency to neuter everything: trying to persuade us of planetary chaos, it incorporates our possible death into everyday blandness. It would like to wake us up, and instead it puts us to sleep. Climatic phenomena, volcanic eruptions, accidents, terrorist attacks, lend our calm existence an unexpected thrill. The enemies are among us and alert to our slightest weaknesses, and are all the more insidious because they are hidden. If the function of ancient rites was to get rid of a community's violence by loading it onto a scapegoat, the function of our contemporary rites is to dramatize the status quo and to make us live in the exciting proximity of a cataclysm. To sound the alarm is to re-enchant the routine under the sign of danger.

In wealthy countries, there is a staggering contrast between the progress achieved and the way people describe themselves. In Europe, we live better than people do elsewhere, despite the economic crisis. But we have never vilified our societies to such a degree. That is the paradox that we have to think about.[3] The voluptuous pleasure of the state of siege: if a flu virus or a few additional degrees in temperature suffice to put whole populations on a war footing, that is because our modern passion for security needs a catastrophe to strengthen itself. In the guise of regularity, our daily grind is supposed to be an absolute disorder that has to be done away with. Thus it is raised to the status of a crime against life: taking a bath or driving a 4×4 become very harmful acts whose consequences can extend as far as the stratosphere. In this case, the deception consists in conferring on everyday matters like eating and lodging the same destructive potential as the atom bomb. It tells each of us: you are potential nuclear warheads. Chernobyl (1986), followed by Fukushima (2011), revealed that nuclear power involves uncontrollable risks. Consider what Günther Anders says about this, with his usual understatement:

> Supporters of nuclear energy, but also and especially supporters of breeder reactors and factories for processing waste, are in no way better than President Truman when he ordered the bombing of Hiroshima. They are even worse, because today people know much more than the naïve president could know in his time. They know what they are doing; he did not.[4]

One can be suspicious regarding the security of our nuclear power plants, and one can desire a gradual abandonment of this mode of energy generation, but one cannot sincerely confuse thermonuclear bombs created to annihilate whole continents with civilian power stations that have been providing light and heating for the past half-century. In this regard, the incredible controversy over the number of Chernobyl's victims proves that the radiation also affected the brains of some commentators: 212 dead according to the World Health Organization, 200,000 according to Greenpeace, nine million according to Corinne Lepage.[5] Nine million, that's a genocide, that's serious stuff!

Does it show discernment to make our societies seem uglier than they are? As we have seen, apocalyptic propaganda is itself the best antidote to the persuasive power of its slogans. The anxiety that it inculcates collapses like a bad soufflé. The last word is had by uneasiness or rather by the panicked will to do away with the risk by any means. Prophets reduce uncertainty: not content to conflate accident and catastrophe, they always offer the same answers to all questions. Consider Fukushima: the tragedy merely confirms a concern that preceded it and was looking for something to justify itself. It was like the Dreyfus Affair for the extreme right in France, 'a divine surprise': finally we had our tragedy! The fear is permanent, its object is purely contingent; yesterday it was the Millennium Bug, today it is global warming and nuclear energy, tomorrow it will be something else. This alarmism is as lazy as naïve optimism and no less illusory. The adepts of the worst-case scenario are still the victims of a fantasy of omnipotence: for them, to prognosticate a hateful destiny is to ward it off. It is one thing to teach the science of catastrophes as a science of reacting to and resisting disproportionate misfortunes; it is another to believe that we will be able to cope with mistakes by forecasting them. We find here an echo of the Stoic practice of *praemeditatio*, the foreseeing of possible future evils in order to evade them. According to Seneca, depriving ourselves of food, subjecting ourselves to cold, hunger, and physical pain, will attenuate the shock of these trials when we have to face them by making us experience misfortune in homeopathic doses. But we are always surprised precisely by what we have foreseen: death, illness, and sorrow crush us anyway, even though we have anticipated them.

On the level of collective action, we cannot predict the magnitude of the turbulences we will encounter. We can prevent their arrival by means of certain appropriate responses. The policies for managing emergencies in the event of industrial crises, hurricanes, forest fires, earthquakes, or enemy attacks have as their goal to propose a range of rapid responses to avoid being taken unprepared and made powerless: mobilizing civil defence forces, the police, even the army. In this domain there is nothing worse than hesitation or tergiversation on the part of the authorities such as we saw in the case of the Bush administration at the time of Hurricane Katrina. We expect our officials to respond immediately to a collective disaster with great words and great acts. We will never forgive a government for not reacting effectively to a public calamity. The right to make mistakes is not granted in this domain, where prediction is nonetheless the least reliable and can fail in two ways: by underestimating threats or by overestimating them, as in the case of the A(H1N1) flu virus. Preparing for something that is difficult to predict: that is the grandeur and the tragedy of the politician. We can protect ourselves by careful planning, rational development of our territory, refusing to grant construction permits in flood zones, on the slopes of volcanoes, in avalanche corridors, and in regions with great seismic activity, as well as by establishing emergency intervention forces. It is better that public authorities err out of excessive concern than out of blind credulity, whereas, inversely, in human relationships trust must be dominant, whatever contingent betrayals may occur. But a hurricane, an epidemic, or a terrorist attack are always haunted by the spectre of their aggravation, and they bear a potential for abominations that the mind cannot envisage without trembling.[6] It takes very little for an assassination to degenerate into a massacre, or a volcanic eruption into absolute devastation. What would have happened had the September 11 attackers succeeded in their plan, or if all the nuclear plants in Japan had been simultaneously affected by the earthquake that occurred in the spring of 2011? Then we would have seen rapidly spreading contagion, certain terror, and annihilation on a grand scale, insofar as in an overpopulated world, the number of victims quickly rises into the thousands or even tens of thousands, as it did in Haiti during the 2010 earthquake.

By means of words, Hannah Arendt wrote, humans can always protect themselves against the blows inflicted by fate: that is the basis of Greek tragedy. Noble phrases respond to the most terrible sufferings and rise to the dignity of action.[7] But how can we protect ourselves when we revel in formulas that are as empty as they are dreadful, when the very heart of language itself is affected? Then the disaster is no longer that of the planet but that of the intelligence. The obsession with security at any price petrifies us, and we increase our fear by trying to eliminate risk. That is what is ridiculous about the great outcries in the media: we wake up in order to demand more passivity, a better protected life. The challenge is not only to decrease the amount of space the media devote to hazards but also to increase our ability to resist misfortunes. To augment our endurance rather than our panic.

The art of distracting attention

In this rhetorical intoxication, the future becomes again, as it had once been in Christianity and communism, the great category of blackmail. The Catholic religion asked us to sacrifice our present joys for the sake of gaining eternal life, while Marxism asked us to forget our bourgeois happiness and embrace instead the classless society. Ecology calls upon us to adopt a rigorous diet in the name of future generations. Once again, it is the German philosopher Hans Jonas who has formulated this idea theoretically by inventing the concept of 'anticipatory remorse'. Our technological and scientific power so far outstrips our knowledge that we are forced to imagine all the wrongs that we might inflict on our descendants by living as we do. The argument is at once brilliant and tortuous: the wrong that I would do the future counts more than human suffering in the present. Up to now, remorse concerned only wrongs already done; with Jonas, it concerns sins to be committed in the future. '[Later men] will in their time have the right to accuse us who came before them of being the originators of their misfortune – if we have spoiled for them the world or the human constitution through careless and avoidable deeds.'[8]

Thus we have to hobble ourselves in order to inhibit our possible cruelty. The future, erected into a tribunal, adjures us to cease destroying the conditions of life on Earth. Screenwriters know this procedure, to which they have given the English name of 'flash-forward', as opposed to 'flash-back': spectators are permitted to glimpse a few minutes of what is to come in order to increase their appetite for it. Leaving our great-grand-children a viable world means postulating that humanity will still exist in coming centuries, and judging our current behaviour from the point of view of future generations. This obligation is based on an ethics of non-reciprocity: we owe our descendants everything without their owing us anything in return. They incarnate a sacred duty which we have no right to evade.

In Christianity, the believer was compelled to choose between salvation and damnation; with Jonas, we have to put ourselves in Hell, mentally, so that our children don't sink into it! A curious inversion: the past remains open, but the future is written in the worst way, as an 'undesirable possibility'. We have to repent in advance for what might happen after us, in a sort of anticipatory sadism. We have to put Prometheus in a straitjacket!

Worrying about what does not yet exist, is that a gesture of love or the worst kind of argument putting pressure on the living, an excess of scrupulous conscience? For fear of soiling our hands, we prefer to cut them off right now. When some people suggest a possible 'juridical asymmetry' in favour of our descendants because of technological risks,[9] they are raising a major philosophical problem: how far can responsibility go without turning into an abstraction? To extend it to all coming generations is to empty it of its meaning, to put a titanic weight on our shoulders. By being accountable for everything, we are accountable for nothing. We can receive no pardon for our errors, since those who would be in a position to grant it have not yet been born! A vicious circle: isn't sacrificing people today for the benefit of those to come also a way of penalizing the latter, especially if we renounce procreation?

Pierre Rosanvallon suggests that we create an Academy of the Future composed of scientists, philosophers, and representatives of associations charged with preventing irreversible degradations: a noble initiative, but one that might end up resembling a spirit circle. Every time, it is spectres born of our fears that are called upon to appear. With Ouija boards, we invoke dead dear ones; in the new academy, it would be those who are not yet born who are vegetating in limbo. Apart from the fact that there are at least two futures – one proximate, that of our children and grandchildren, over whom we still have some power, and a distant one that is beyond our control – no one can rule on the future because doing so would essentially make our intellectual frameworks outdated and exceed the very conditions of our knowledge.[10] Tocqueville suspected this: in a democracy, he wrote, every generation is a new nation, and tradition is less an imperative than a source of information. It is true that a choice made freely by one generation becomes the destiny of the next, and that we experience our predecessors' options as a calamity: for example, the post-war architecture that invaded and disfigured the whole planet. But we act first of all on what depends on us, on that with which we can establish connections. Exhausting ourselves trying to imagine the craziest scenarios for tomorrow – a bacterial infection, computer bugs, intergalactic wars, meteorological or nuclear cataclysms, falling asteroids – and sacrificing everything to the conceptual ectoplasm of 'future generations' is to buy a conscience on the cheap and to close one's eyes to present scandals.

As Rimbaud said, we have to become seers, but in a more prosaic way: 'An individual who wants to grasp the gravity of a problem like climate change must look very far beyond his preferences, his family, his home, his comfort.'[11] A rehabilitation of small trades, tea-leaf readers, fortune-tellers: we must all become eagle-eyed on our own levels. 'Make invisible evil visible,' Ivan Illich said. So be it! But who are the superior beings capable of seeing what others do not, of scenting potential danger in the most cheerful places? Diviners endowed with a special empathy? This distant other is a temporal phantom that makes it possible to put actual others between parentheses. The 'destiny that eyes us from the future' makes us neglect our duties to those close to us. Third-Worldism stressed the crimes of colonialism in order to avoid speaking about the crimes of the decolonized; ecologists, wholly absorbed in their science-fiction ethics, care more about our possible misdeeds than about present injustices. Beneath the ingenuity of the prophecy, propaganda is pulling hidden strings to distract attention from today's problems. For everyone, there are five major scourges: hunger, poverty, disease, natural disasters, mass killings. For the classic questions of justice, equality, and security, ecology substitutes, in the name of the 'planet,' a single imperative: survival.

> Capitalists may be wearing blinders, obsessed as they are by short-term profit, but they cannot ignore the uneasiness that wealthy nations are showing with regard to their future. Climatic, energy, atomic, and technological threats are worrying people and transforming passive consumers into citizens who ask themselves: why continue along the same road if it is leading us to the abyss? [. . .] if the Brazilian or Chinese 'miracles' continue, we will all go down together.[12]

The expert has spoken: let the Brazilians, Indians, and Chinese resign themselves to rotting away in their mire, the salvation of the planet is at stake. Too bad about those starving bastards who'd like to improve their fates a bit! Putting the Earth back on track is well worth sacrificing a few billion Asians and South Americans.

Thus it takes the imminence of an infinite calamity to redeem the human adventure. On this level our age testifies to a narcissism of malediction that rips it out of its insignificance and reaffirms its centrality: by designating itself as damned, it merely emphasizes its singularity while apparently depreciating itself: 'Our period is not accidentally ephemeral; ephemerality is its essence. It cannot pass into another period but only collapse.'[13]

What a relief to know that we are not living in a little province of time but in the historic moment when time itself is going to be engulfed! What presumption, and what naïveté, to believe that we are at the pinnacle of history! This self-abasement is a form of vainglory. If we can't be the best, we can still be the worst. Behind their lamentations, the catastrophists are bursting with self-importance.

The breast-beaters

Since the age of Enlightenment, European intellectuals have fulfilled three functions: criticism of the prejudices of their times, pathfinders for collective action, and guides for a party or a camp. In the nineteenth century a fourth function was added, that of a secular prophet, a pastor for the people, invested with a spiritual power: intellectuals tell their period truths it does not want to hear. Intellectuals thus became rebels who rise up and visionaries who foresee. In classical Judaism, the prophet espoused the cause of God against kings and the powerful. Abolishing any distinction between the spiritual and the temporal, the prophet sought to establish an authentic community in this world and not in the next.[14] In Christianity, millenarian uprisings carried within them a hope for justice against the Church, which was betraying the poor and the Gospels by wallowing in luxury.[15] These uprisings, which were harshly repressed, promised a world without violence in which the lion and the lamb would lie down together, and where the Lord would 'wipe away all the tears from their eyes' (The Apocalypse According to St John).

In a secular society, the prophet is no longer an intercessor between God and humans: he is inhabited by a moral certainty and has no viaticum other than his indignation. He raises up the masses by his charisma, creates an 'emotional community' (Max Weber) in order to blaze new paths in a fixed history. But sometimes, intoxicated by his own words, he arrogates to himself an undeserved legitimacy and calls for the destruction that he claims to reject.[16] This is the reversal: for its partisans, the Apocalypse becomes our only chance for salvation. If in Catholicism eschatology is the science of last things, catastrophism is the narrative of the 'last end', so to speak, after which there will be nothing. Like the reactionaries who in the 1960s and 1970s hoped for

a good war that would calm down the young, catastrophists hope that we will touch bottom in order to
wake us up. You deserve a good lesson, you haven't
suffered enough, you need to have a hard time of it. It
is a genuine death wish that they address to people:
punishment is in itself a kind of redemption.

Thus there are two distinct kinds of pessimism: a
cultural pessimism that holds up a mirror to societies
and points out their moral debasement when they show
themselves inferior to the values they proclaim, and an
anthropological pessimism that condemns the human
race, which is forever fallen. The prophet is not a great
soul who admonishes us but a petty fellow who wishes
us many misfortunes if we have the gall not to listen
to him. Catastrophe is not something that haunts him
but his source of joy. For him, it does not suffice to
inundate us with gloomy analyses and desperate obser-
vations: from the depths of his bitterness, he wants to
convince us, to win disciples. He takes his disenchantment very seriously. Disaster fascinates some minds
because it has a clarifying effect: it cuts history in two,
tears it away from the indetermination of the everyday
where things are neither completely good nor completely bad. Rather chaos than indecision. Just as in
literature there are tourists of genocide – such as we see
in Jonathan Littel's *The Kindly Ones*, for instance – who
take pleasure in atrocities and wallow in blood, in philosophy there are calamity lovers who travel the globe
sniffing carnage and impregnating themselves with its
atmosphere.

In May 1897 the Bazar de la Charité, a building
housing a Catholic high society welfare organization in
Paris, burned down after an ether lamp set a curtain on
fire. In the confusion, more than a hundred people died,
almost all of them aristocratic women. It was a terrible
tragedy that decimated the nobility. Léon Bloy, a now
forgotten Catholic pamphleteer, published an inflamma-
tory epistle in which he expressed his delight at the fire,

seeing in it the hand of God taking revenge on the materialism and irreligion of the period in France. The collocation of the words 'bazaar' and 'charity' deserved the most pitiless punishment. His only regret? That there had not been more victims. Our period is full of people like Léon Bloy, who rejoice as they await the Deluge: they would like to see at least three Fukushimas a year. It is a short step from lucidity to bitterness, from foresightedness to the spirit of revenge. Accompanied by a whole tribe of magi and raving prophetesses, our vaticinators curse the careless masses and wish them great woe. Excellent minds can qualify and refute all they want, our courtiers of the Last Judgment refuse to listen to them. Maybe here we need to invert the proposition: *it could be that ecology, as a discourse, seeks not so much to save us from the end of the world as to precipitate it. It is both the agent and the vehicle of our death wish.* If it is more flourishing in Europe than anywhere else, that is because some people in the European elites no longer want to live and desire our disappearance. The radical ecologists are providing us with palliative care, so to speak, before we are swallowed up forever. In a brilliant study already cited, Jared Diamond has shown how certain societies – the Mayas, the Vikings, Easter Islanders, among others – collaborated in their own ruin.[17] A nation or a group of nations can choose failure, deliberately, out of self-hatred.

What, then, is the right distance between reasonable warning and sterile panic? Every critical remark that violates a consensus and the law of silence is in principle untimely. But when the consensus involves general despair, when a whole society speaks with a single voice full of imprecations, when day and night the media inventory with a maniacal precision all the shapes taken by devastation, criticism is transformed into drivel. We need to think about the recurrence of catastrophes in the media, year after year. Epidemics, natural phenomena, viruses, and industrial accidents punctuate our everyday life with the regularity of a metronome and provoke injections of collective fear followed by a period of calm before the next peak. According to one historian, since Nostradamus we have escaped 183 ends of the world,[18] and over the past dozen years at least five have been counted: in 1999 the astrologist Elizabeth Teissier warned that the Cassini orbiter would crash to Earth on 24 July; the fashion designer Paco Rabanne feared that the Russian space station *Mir* would devastate Paris on 11 August of the same year, the day of a total eclipse of the sun; still in 1999, the philosopher Paul Virilio predicted a computer bug when the year 2000 arrived; in 2008, the start-up of the giant CERN particle collider near Geneva caused many scientists to fear the formation of a black hole that would dislocate the universe (two ecologists filed a suit in Honolulu to force the United States to withdraw its support for the project); finally, Pastor Harold Camping, the leader of a Protestant sect, predicted that New Zealand and Australia would sink into the ocean on 21 May 2011. Better luck next time!

There are at least two types of Cassandras. On the one hand, there are those who deduce an imminent danger from a precise situation, like Maurice Allais's doubts about the euro in 2004 or Nouriel Roubini predicting in 2006 a collapse of the American real estate market. And on the other hand, there are those who scorn us, like the prophet Philippulus in Hergé's *L'Étoile mystérieuse*, who announces the end of time by striking a gong because a meteorite is approaching the Earth (according to recognized experts on Tintin, Philippulus is a caricature of Marshal Pétain demanding, as soon as he took power, that the French repent for imaginary sins).[19] In the case of the financial crisis, the carelessness with which things went back to business as usual augurs ill for the future: a society that fails to learn from its errors dooms itself not only to repeating them but also to exacerbating them. What can we reply to a people who promise you the Cataclysm with the amazing calm of fanatics? Who devote their days and nights to *preaching the gospel of despair*? We can only shrug our shoulders. They are irrefutable, because their propositions are 'unfalsifiable'. The apostles of fear believe in their phobias and are interested solely in spreading their discouragement everywhere. The success of gloomy prophecy, at least in the media, follows a twentieth century marked by totalitarian catastrophes, Nazism and communism taken together. We are heirs to a double disaster, Auschwitz and Hiroshima: in one case an orgy of industrially planned hatred, in the other nuclear bombs dropped without hatred on civilian populations in order to force Japan to surrender. Our task is to understand both of these. Just as no one wanted to believe or even conceive the mass murder undertaken by the Nazis, any more than the Soviet and Maoist gulags, now we compete in imagining the dreadful in order to prevent its return. Let us note that three of the major crimes of the post-war period were committed with rudimentary technology: the Cambodian auto-genocide, using pickaxes and plastic bags (to save on munitions); the genocide of the Tutsis in Rwanda, using machetes; the hijacking of aeroplanes on September 11, using box cutters held at the pilot's throats. And each time, we were stunned by what happened, which upset all our calculations.

Radical ecology does not fall into the same trap as Marxism did: promising paradise on Earth. It limits itself to denouncing the Hell of our societies. Not being bound by any precise calendar, it eludes the test of verification. Since ecosystems take centuries to respond to the damage done them, we will no longer be here to see whether the predictions of radical ecology are right or wrong. Our harbingers of doom win in any case. If nothing happens, they will claim it is because of them. A marvellous dialectic: the success of the prediction, the irruption of the dreaded trauma, would be a misfortune, but failure is in fact a success, misfortune averted. To win would be to lose, but to lose is to win. 'The prophecy of doom is made to avert its coming, and it would be the height of injustice later to deride the "alarmists" because "it did not turn out so bad after all." To have been wrong may be their merit.'[20]

What most distressed biblical oracles was that people acted on them (that is the tragedy of Jonah, who prophesied that God would destroy Nineveh and was angry with him for having changed his mind after the people of the city repented). They needed to remain marginal and alone to brandish the radicalness of their Word. Contemporary augurs are consulted and remain privileged even if what they say is rapidly drowned in the babble of the media. The Christian Apocalypse presented itself as a revelation, a passage into another temporal order, whereas this apocalypse reveals nothing, it issues the final judgment: pure apocalypse. No promise of redemption, just an ideal for survivors, an 'epidemic of remorse', a coming together of hundreds of millions of people who are repenting and trying to escape chaos. How can we be surprised when so many lofty minds go off the rails, when the most aberrant predictions flourish, like the one based on the Mayan calendar that predicted the end of the world in December 2012? The whole surface of the Earth was supposed to disappear except for a small village in southern France, Bugarach, population 200, which would be taken over by all the planet's enlightened ones. Armageddon is imminent. We dream of Job and Jeremiah and end up with Paco Rabanne!

France, the Fecund Depression

The strikes that took place in France during the autumn of 2010 provided the astonishing spectacle of secondary school students demonstrating to preserve their retirement pensions. A strange inversion: before they have even begun their working life, these teenagers going grey at the temples are already thinking about ending it. The future has to be written in advance and life made secure from the cradle to the grave. One thinks of the stupefying poll published a few years ago showing that in France 70 per cent of those under thirty yearned for risk-free careers as government officials. The young, who have been hard hit by unemployment, are in the van of the largest party in France, the party of fear. The French are afraid of the world, of insecurity, of others, and they are still more afraid of their fear, which spreads among them with the celerity of a lightning bolt. It is a fear that is maintained day after day by the media and the elites, and that proceeds from our inability to find our bearings in a universe that has become too complex. The French passion for strikes, our national sport, is less a sign of vitality than a sign of routine, a fine example of a conquest that has become a symptom of depression. Didn't Olivier Besancenot (a far-left candidate for president in 2007 and the spokesman for the New Anti-Capitalist Party from 2009 to 2011) propose in 2003 to create a great strike party? Schoolchildren would be able to join it before they had held any post at all. Since our country has long since ceased to be the 'indispensable nation', we have to go on strike against the outside world, to exorcize this pressure exerted by all on all that we call globalization. We expect work stoppages in each season, in railway stations, public transportation, and airports, as we expect autumn, with a mixture of fatalism and excitement. In this routine rebellion there is anxiety but there is also the foot-stamping of the spoiled child.

The French, who are past masters in the art of overestimating themselves, are also Europe's greatest consumers of tranquillizers and other psychotropic drugs. The centre of villages is no longer the church or the city hall, but the pharmacy. France has to rhyme with *souffrance* (suffering) with *déchéance* (decline); we are never recognized, loved, coddled enough. The whole country is one immense association of complainers, and we give our slightest difficulties the fantastic character of tragedies. We are afflicted with a psychic weariness, an inability to surmount adversity that increases our weakness. Hence the French dream of a frozen, hermetically sealed life that sees rich and poor closing themselves off in their communes, their neighbourhoods, and their ghettos, like Asterix in his village. That is also why so many young people, smothered by this national closedness, are leaving France for other horizons, America, Asia, Africa. Were it only a minuscule canton prey to the torments of the age, France, that universal gadfly that meddles in everything that does not concern it, that hedonist land that is fanatical about vacations and has invented a culture of pleasures unique in the world, would be one metaphor among others of the decline of Europe. Our country, which was classified at the end of 2010 among the most pessimistic nations, well ahead of Iraq, Afghanistan, and Nigeria, nonetheless also has one of the highest birth rates in the Old World, all classes taken together, thanks to a policy that favours families and makes it possible for French women to combine work with maternity. A strange form of schizophrenia: it is as if we were fighting our own pessimism by refilling our cradles. As if in each French person two distinct beings cohabited, one that moans and another that procreates: the former concludes that the end of the world is nigh, while the other thinks it is living at the beginning of a new era. Not without narcissism, we delegate to our children the hope that has left us, and we connect up again with that most ancient act: giving birth. That is, with the faculty of beginning over, the opportunity offered each generation to cast an astonished look on this Earth and to launch out – why not? – with renewed enthusiasm. That is how the dialectic between protection and the taste for adventure is resolved.

Part II

Progressives Against Progress

4

The Last Avatar of Prometheus?

For the past few centuries, every increase in productive capacity has been accompanied by growth in destructive capacity.

Raymond Aron, preface to Max Weber's
Le Savant et le politique, 1959

In an apocryphal gospel, the Apocalypse of Stephen, which has never been authenticated or integrated into the Protestant or Catholic canons, Noah, as he is loading his animals onto the Ark, is alarmed by the large number of candidates. Mammals, birds, marsupials, penguins, primates, and lizards have already gone on board. The ass, the ox, the giraffe, the elk, the stag, the lion, and the cat urge the patriarch to raise the gangplank and close the hatches. The boat is chock-full, the cedar hull is about to crack open, the Deluge is threatening. Outside, a crowd of harmful or misshapen pests – cockroaches, toads, slugs, spiders – asks to be taken on. The toad speaks on behalf of his unsightly comrades: he pleads their cause with eloquence, pointing out to the Patriarch that they perform a useful function in nature.

In God's designs, nothing is ugly or repugnant: everything is ingenious, even invertebrates and molluscs are necessary. No one has the right to destroy these creatures of the Lord. But Noah turns on his heel and decides to raise anchor. Then a cloud of insects and pests assails him: fleas climb on his legs, crabs crawl in his pubic hair, crab lice swarm on his head, leeches, stinkbugs, and mosquitoes stick to his skin without him noticing them. Snakes slip into his flowing hair, spiders take up residence in his beard. That is how the whole inferior bestiary was spared.

Today, who would not dream of taking on board a giant Ark, rocket ship or space shuttle, the tens of millions of surviving species, whether vegetable or animal, in order to save them from human rapacity and to deposit them on a planet where they could develop without constraint?

The inevitability of forward movement

The case against progress is as old as the idea of progress itself. Rousseau, a contemporary of the first steam engines, lambasts the discovery of iron and the cultivation of wheat; the prisons imagined by Piranesi (1720–78), with their pulleys, terrifying vaults, flights of stairs, and instruments of torture, sketch out the gigantic dungeon that Enlightenment thinkers built in spite of themselves while trying to extricate themselves from the obscurity of the *Ancien Régime*.[1] Mary Shelley published her *Frankenstein* in 1818, right in the middle of the Saint-Simonian euphoria. In the nineteenth century, according to a line of criticism initiated by the Frankfurt School and further developed by Jacques Ellul and Ivan Illich, humanity's triumphal march toward improvement is self-contradictory in its ambitions: medicine kills us and produces new pathologies, school produces mass ignorance, food makes us obese, transportation separates people as much as it brings them together. This is the reign of general counter-productiveness: 'The corruption of the best gives rise to the worst' (Ivan Illich). Nonetheless, progress's main crime is to have freed the demon of immoderation that lives within us, the evil genius of omnipotence. That is why, according to Illich, peaceful industrial enterprises have become as destructive as world wars: they reawaken the unhealthy dream of being a god.

> With the industrialization of desire, hubris has become collective and society is the material realization of the nightmare. Industrial hubris has broken the mythical frame that set limits to the madness of dreams [. . .]. The ineluctable backlash of material progress is Nemesis for the masses, the naked material monster born from the industrial dream.[2]

Beyond a certain critical threshold, the most effective systems are transformed into highly undesirable configurations and turn against their users in order to destroy them.

Walter Benjamin reports that in 1848 French rebels fired on clocks to protest against the tyranny of schedules. In 1909, Marinetti published a futurist manifesto entitled *Uccidiamo il chiaro di luna* (*Let's Kill the Moonlight*) and professed a violent hatred of nature and women; today, at the initiative of the Czech Republic, some countries are thinking about turning off municipal lighting at night in order to preserve the darkness and the beauty of the stars.[3] Three stages: the revolt against capitalism's segmentation of time, a violent taste for artifice, and finally the refusal of the electricity that blinds us to the night while trying to enlighten us. If progress continues, it has been demoted to an automatic invention: we have lost the Enlightenment hope of

reconciling the advance of humanity's moral improvement with the advance of prosperity and learning. We
have become richer and better educated, but we have
not become better. The twentieth century is said to have
pushed barbarism to an unequalled level in the Nazi
death camps and the Soviet, Chinese, and Cambodian
gulags. Didn't Heidegger declare, in a talk given in 1949
to minimize his adherence to National Socialism, that
motorized agriculture and 'the production of corpses'
in Auschwitz were one and the same thing?[4] Progress is
now the object of an ambiguous cult; it is less a hope
than an established fact, the lot of a society that produces, whatever happens, its quota of novelties and
gadgets in all domains. Progressivism, that is, the belief
in the virtues of the future, is at once a kind of combat
and a recognition: it is a mixture of voluntarism and
following the herd. Movement for movement's sake,
that is what remains of this hope, which has become the
height of conformism. And like the Red Queen in
Through the Looking-Glass, we are forced to run constantly just to stay where we are. We move in order to
remain immobile. Who is not a progressive in this
respect, even on the right, conservative in manners but
a fervent adept of technological upheavals? Our constant movement carries us away and increasingly resembles relentless change. The festival of progress never
stops; it spares us the twofold impasse of anxiety: there
is no void and no saturation because desire is constantly
renewed. Instead of striding rapidly down the paths to
the future, we bend under the inertia of inevitable
change. There is a curse in this forward movement,
which tolerates no pause, no going back. 'There will
always remain something disconcerting', Kant said, 'in
the fact that earlier generations wanted to devote all
their effort solely to the benefit of later generations
[. . .], in such way that the later generations alone would
have the good fortune to inhabit the edifice already
completed.'[5] But in this edifice, water is polluted, air is

unbreathable, nature is devastated, and the current generation curses its forebears for having bequeathed it a poisoned gift.

Intermittent lights

Worse yet: new problems keep sprouting, like the heads of the legendary Hydra. Hardly have we dealt with one focus of pain before another springs up, making our efforts seem ridiculous. An enemy we thought we had conquered continues to hurt us; undeniable victories, the eradication of a certain number of diseases that had been relegated to the past, have been put in question by the return of old viruses or bacilli in more aggressive forms, not to mention the appearance of new, ultra-resistant bacteria against which our antibiotics are powerless. We are not moving from the darkness toward the light, as nineteenth-century positivists had thought; we are only redistributing darkness and light in a different way. And since we cannot predict the long-term effects of our inventions, we have to show restraint when putting into circulation a new molecule or genetically modified seed. A present decision, made carelessly, could affect the survival of humanity. Our responsibility includes not only the extent of what we know but also the greater expanse of what we do not know. Whence the potentially tragic character of any innovation, which can, 'in a sort of retroactive revelation' (François Ewald),[6] conceal a problem that we neither foresaw nor intended. This new kind of risk upsets the order of time and makes us criminals who have committed no crime, since we cannot know the consequences of our acts. In other words, because we have disciplined nature as much as we have ravaged it, we have become co-responsible for it: its fate coincides with our own. Our partial mastery of nature makes us its debtors, and our debt is redeemed by an endless dispossession.

Science used to seek to emancipate humanity from the tyranny of matter. The latter constituted an unlimited reservoir of ores, fossil energies, and animal and vegetable species to be appropriated. But nature has in turn entered into the order of finitude; it has ceased to be inexhaustible. The problem is complicated by the fact that the instruments of our domination over nature have become the instruments of technology's domination over us: according to Heidegger's analysis, technology is no longer a means to an end but our destiny, a process that we can no longer stop but at most slow down. An unprecedented power concentrated in the hands of human beings goes hand in hand with the impossibility of curbing that power. By trying to free ourselves from natural constraints, we have put ourselves under the yoke of a new master, machines which, in their extreme sophistication, exceed our understanding. Thus some people foresee a network of computers endowed with artificial intelligence that will someday take power over us. If, for Francis Bacon (1561–1626), the object of science was to restore humanity's authority over the world after the Fall, he was in this case squarely in the Judeo-Christian tradition: humans' opportunity to exploit so-called inferior species went hand-in-hand with a duty to treat them with kindness and compassion. On this point, Christianity was more anthropocentric than Judaism, which included animals as members of the covenant with God.[7]

The fear of seeing humans hold nature under their power remains very largely a fiction. Our sovereignty over things is both excessive and incomplete. We have sufficient means to destroy the world from top to bottom, notably in the nuclear domain, but they are not great enough to bend it to our will. The Earth has been partly devastated, but we have in no way tamed it, as is proven by volcanic eruptions, tornados, seismic events, and meteorological aberrations. *Humans are intermittent and pathetic demiurges.*

Do we control the weather?

For the past two decades we have been experiencing a major epistemological event: there are no longer any natural catastrophes. Tsunamis in Southeast Asia and Japan, earthquakes in Chile, Italy, and Haiti, storms in western France, more severe winters, torrid summers – all these are supposed to be of human origin. At the very time that we are trying to humble human pride, we are imputing to ourselves all imaginable kinds of damage. Nothing happens without a reason; there are no longer any accidents, only the consequences, voluntary or involuntary, of our seizure of control over the planet. Walking on the Earth, we see everywhere only our work, the mirror of our acts. And the dangers that we believe are natural – submarine commotions, a kind of epilepsy of the planet's crust, erosions, hurricanes – are our own avatars, returning like boomerangs to strike us. Thus, the new orthodoxy tells us, for the past ten years we have been experiencing a spectacular increase in catastrophes. Isn't it rather our sensitivity to climatic disturbances that has become exacerbated?[8] Whereas the twentieth century still saw tidal waves and earthquakes as random events, we now see them as effects of our own actions. In every natural scourge we are on the lookout for a future disaster: the slightest difference in temperature or slippage in the terrain foretells a disastrous event. We are in the implacable logic of the countdown. We no longer have the right to be careless; crises are accumulating. We await the final spasm as others await the return of the Messiah. In 2000, a British journalist went so far as to write, referring to Britain: 'Snowfalls are now just a thing of the past.'[9] We are still waiting for an explanation or at least excuses . . .

What is a catastrophe, from this point of view? A semantic framework that lends meaning to

incomprehensible events. Consider this reflection by
Anthony Giddens and Martin Rees, writing about the
events of 2010:

> No-one can say with certainty that events such as the
> flooding in Pakistan, the unprecedented weather
> episodes in some parts of the US, the heat-wave and
> drought in Russia, or the floods and landslides in
> Northern China, were influenced by climate change. Yet
> they constitute a stark warning. Extreme weather events
> will grow in frequency and intensity as the world
> warms.[10]

This is a semantic move typical of the new ideology
that explains all phenomena by a hypothesis: 'No one
can say . . .', but we say it. Interpretation is twisted in
order to awaken the audience from its torpor. The procedure is patently dishonest, but it is adopted with the
best intentions. In the Middle Ages, natural cataclysms
were interpreted as divine punishments, a notion that is
preserved in the legal expression 'act of God'. In the
fourteenth century, for instance, earthquakes that
occurred in Italy and Carinthia, and especially the Black
Death epidemic, were seen by millenarian sects as the
'Messianic sufferings' preceding the Last Days, a terrible
trial to be endured before humanity's redemption.[11] But
at that time, insecurity and famine were causing escha-
tological fever to peak. Misfortunes were attributed to
the human creature's impotence. Today they are attributed to our excessive power, even though we benefit, at
least in developed countries, from an increased life
expectancy and an abundant food supply unprecedented
in history.

The ancients used chicken entrails or the flights of
birds to divine the future. We scrutinize the sky to read
in it the signs of our destiny: what isn't global warming
in this respect? Rain is warming, and so is drought, as
well as wind, blizzards, cyclones, even cold, according
to Al Gore's marvellous logical acrobatics:[12] the rise in

temperatures cools us because melting ice packs will halt the Gulf Stream that maintains a temperate climate along the coasts of Europe. In ten years, in twenty years, we will have found another explanation to calm our anxiety. But for the moment this magic skeleton key opens all doors. Besides, if climatic disturbance is a probability, should it be made a priority? Should we spend billions in an effort to counteract its effects instead of using those funds to fight real scourges such as poverty and disease? Do we have to go to great ends to cause temperatures to fall by the most preposterous means – such as disseminating millions of tonnes of sulphate particles in the stratosphere so that they will reflect sunlight, as a Nobel Prize winner in chemistry, Paul Crutzen, recommended – instead of helping the countries and islands threatened by rising sea levels (even if since 1992 that rise has remained remarkably stable, at 3.3 mm per year, despite the melting of the polar icecaps)?[13]

At the same time that humans are being made responsible for all the evils in the universe, human intentions are being attributed to Mother Nature, who is made into an entity endowed with volitions and feelings. Great geological upheavals are to be understood as the revolt of our Mother Earth, who is punishing her children by sending them the seven plagues of Egypt. A strange reversal that reminds us of the Hegelian master-slave dialectic: the alleged omnipotence of human beings is said to be opposed by the fierce resistance of a tortured planet. Mother Earth is dying and we are dying with her; she takes advantage of this to teach us a lesson. Disturbances in the weather foretell our future: they are vectors, predictions sent by the skies to warn us. Trying to illustrate 'the human mind's helplessness confronted by its staggering creations', a didactic journalist writes: 'The slumber of consciousness gives birth to monsters. Time bombs – nuclear, climatic, chemical – are beginning to explode. We're in for it.'[14]

The tsunami of March 2011 and the Fukushima nuclear accident? Humans alone are guilty:

> It's as if Nature were rising up before us and telling us, from the height of its twenty-foot waves: 'You tried to conceal the evil that inhabits you by likening it to my violence. But my violence is pure, and prior to your categories of good and evil. I am punishing you by taking literally your assimilation of your instruments of death with my immaculate power. So perish by the tsunami!'[15]

So now we have the Earth 'avenging' itself! Here, we are completely immersed in black magic: calamities are punishments for human outrageousness. We have to calm the wrath of God or the elements; above all, we need scapegoats, and the principle of imputation desperately seeks them in order to explain the tragedies.

The earthquake that occurred in Haiti in January 2010? That is also our fault because we colonized the island in the nineteenth century, a journalist explains.[16] It is a mystery how the former colonial power that left Haiti in 1825, though not without demanding an iniquitous tribute, could have caused a terrible earthquake 185 years later. During the winter of 2001, in Picardy in northern France, the Somme River overflowed its bed. The people affected by this disaster accused the authorities of the Île-de-France region of having diverted water from the Seine into the Somme to relieve the Paris basin, as one empties a sink! That was the rumour in Abbeville, which forced public authorities to issue a formal denial of the charge. The 2004 tsunami in Southeast Asia was also interpreted as a biblical disaster (when it was not attributed, by certain conspiracy-theory websites, to Zionist or North American forces). It was a good thrashing administered to us by the furious oceans and the angered crust of the Earth: by occupying littoral areas to develop tourism, by destroying the mangroves, intensifying fishing, deforesting the plains and hills to extend livestock-raising areas, humans created the conditions for their death. Nature is like God: it will confirm all kinds of designs, even the most aggressive, and never refute any. According to the most well informed – that is, the most paranoid – capitalism is so Machiavellian that it jumps on natural disasters in order to repair them afterward and to make money on reconstruction, when it does not try to provoke them itself.[17] It pounces on the woes of the world the way the pox pounces on the lower clergy. If for Galileo nature was a book written in a mathematical language, today it is a book written in the esoteric language of conspiracy, of sorcery.

To this excess corresponds what might be called a 'theory of mad causalities': for example, to blame the 15,000 deaths during the heat wave of 2003 on truck traffic on the highways, as Serge Latouche did, is to leave the realm of reason. It is one thing to make 'Danone and other yogurt producers understand the virtues of milk, of cardboard, and the aroma of proximity',[18] and another to accuse them of causing the death of several thousand elderly people in northern France, which was due instead to the negligence of public authorities and healthcare establishments. But every explanation is reassuring at a time when the extreme sophistication of the instruments of knowledge makes climatic phenomena difficult to understand and predict. It is more our inadequacies than our certainties that are confirmed in this way. Mathematically, we are headed for exponential upheavals because there are more people, especially in cities, and they occupy smaller and smaller territories, thus concentrating, in wealthy countries, more added value per square kilometre. In densely populated zones the effects of any natural incident will be multiplied by a lack of preparation on the part of public authorities. *We are experiencing the combined product of the Earth's turmoil and human negligence.* Thus the exceptionally violent earthquake and the subsequent tsunami that took place in Japan in March 2011 and killed at least 30,000 people was accompanied by the incompetence of the nuclear industry, which built reactors on a seismic fault near the ocean. The markers set up by their ancestors, which indicated that houses must not be built less than 800 metres from the coast, were ignored. The magnitude 7 earthquake that struck Haiti, a small, poorly governed country, in January 2010 caused 250,000 deaths. The 8.8 magnitude quake that occurred shortly afterward in Chile, a country that has long since adopted anti-seismic norms, caused 700 deaths.

Hurricane Katrina, which hit New Orleans on 29 August 2005, affected chiefly deprived groups, most of them Black, who were at the mercy of the waters after the levees on the Mississippi and the canals broke (some parts of the city are as much as two metres below sea level). In every democracy, risks, like riches, have to be fairly shared, and this principle was not respected in the present case. It is not correct to say, like the theorist of climatic war Harald Welzer, that 'the hurricane led to a complete collapse of the social order'.[19] Despite the gunshots and the looting and rioting, which are inevitable in this kind of disorder, the evacuation of almost a million residents was achieved one way or another; the victims showed a great mutual solidarity, and as for the violence, it was also committed in part by police forces famous for their corruption and racism,[20] to the point where some signs carried by protestors during demonstrations denouncing the federal authorities' inaction proclaimed, not without derision: 'Buy us Back Chirac!' (Louisiana was French until 1803, when it was sold to the young United States by Napoleon for $15 million).

At a time when demographic pressure is increasing everywhere, we have less than ever any right to be careless in choosing construction materials or avoiding industrial risks. Of course, human responsibility is involved when we confront natural phenomena that are predictable and recurrent. But to extend it to the whole of the planet, and even to the solar system, is as unreasonable as the scientistic will to subjugate matter. We lack the means to command Creation, to cause snow to fall or the sun to shine whenever we wish. The Earth is never angry or happy: it obeys its own laws and we would be wise to learn them, the better to avoid succumbing to them.

The living, a subject with rights?

What characterizes nature? It does not speak, or rather it speaks too much, in obscure messages; it is that 'temple where each living column,/At times, gives forth vague words' (Charles Baudelaire). It expresses itself in countless murmurs that the poet, the scientist, and the herbalist seek to hear and to praise. It is a conversation beyond words that never ceases and is spoken by the blowing of the wind, the rustling of leaves, the patter of rain, the rushing of torrents. To grant the gift of languages to cows, pigs, bears, and trees, as did the ancients and, closer to us, Jean de La Fontaine, Rudyard Kipling, Jules Renard, and Marcel Aymé, is to project our affectivity onto them: 'Gardens speak very little, except in my book,' La Fontaine said. Nature, like God, being mute or excessively loquacious, we have to become its interpreters, just as in his *Theodicy* Leibniz made himself God's advocate in order to justify the order of things. 'We must restore its voice to the world of silence.'[21] The exercise is delicate and demands great talent: what should we have plankton, coral reefs, and marine trenches say, apart from explaining their function, their complexity, and their splendour in the most precise words possible? Properly naming things is no more nor less than endowing them with the right to exist.

The sociologist Bruno Latour proposes, for instance, to establish a 'Senate of the Non-living' in order to expand the field of politics to the Earth as a whole. All right; but who will speak in the name of the planet? Will we see a caste of clerics who will translate the wishes of stones, clay, plants, and adapt cosmic signals, the way there are now experts on UFOs?

'[P]erhaps only a passive franchise for grass and earthworms will bring humanity to its senses' (Ulrich Beck).[22] We have to hope that this is a bit of involuntary humour in a work that is otherwise pertinent. Who will poll the blades of grass, carry their votes to the ballot box, offer them a choice of candidates? Edgar Morin, citing Ernesto Sabato, says that we need 'worldologists' (*mondiologues*), that is, minds capable of synthesizing the whole of our knowledge and data concerning the planet. A noble project, but one that is in danger of arriving at a compilation by autodidacts that would remind us of the burlesque encyclopaedia in Flaubert's *Bouvard et Pécuchet*. We tremble at the idea of a university granting degrees in 'Earthology', producing amiable specialists in vagueness who are capable of discoursing with equal authority on the acidification of the oceans, the disappearance of gray wolves in North America, working conditions in China, the progress of molecular biology, the hypofertility of male earthworms, the spirituality of shamans, and so on. Their incompetence in these domains would be equalled only by their enthusiasm for revealing the most secret mechanisms at work in each of them.

Thus according to the new orthodoxy, there are two ways of reasoning: one that centres on human beings and their welfare, and another that seeks to denounce the primacy of anthropocentrism and to promote an 'animal ethics' that is 'biocentric' or even 'ecospheric', i.e. that includes the totality of living beings.[23] Why not?

To humble human presumption, to make us no longer the lords of the world but its inhabitants among others, has also been for several centuries the task of a certain kind of philosophy. But 'thinking like a mountain', to borrow the lovely expression coined by Aldo Leopold (1887–1948), defending the nobility of trees as a heritage to be preserved, making rivers speak, granting legal status to a plain or a quarry, is never anything more than a way of shifting the problem. Do natural beings, animals, have the right to have rights? No doubt, because they suffer just as we do and want to enjoy their being. But these are in any case derived rights, of which humanity is the sole guarantor: the specific characteristic of a subject with rights is first of all the ability to defend them. This is the case with neither animals nor plants: they can inspire our pity, move us, but they cannot plead their cases except through the mediation of human beings sensitive to their condition. Must we grant rights to humanoids, to automatons, draw up a 'Bill of Rights for Robots', as South Korea has proposed? But if they're autonomous, then it's up to them to seize these rights![24] Nor is it more convincing to object that we give rights to beings that are unconscious or incapable of independence – foetuses, newborns, slaves, the dying, and the mentally ill. The foetus will become capable of speech and independence, the slave can be emancipated and become a free individual, and as for those who are in comas, they have been healthy beings even if their condition has deteriorated. The fact that we are only a 'fragment of the world' (Stéphane Ferret) is not new, but ours is the only species that demands to be considered one among others. Who defends the right of forests and cliffs if not some human beings against others? To assimilate speciesism to sexism, to write, for example, that 'Animals are meat, guinea pigs for experiments and objectified bodies; women are treated like meat, like guinea pigs and objectified bodies,' is to force interpretation to a grotesque degree.[25] So far as I know, women are not devoured on spits. Anyone who confuses his wife with a piece of roast beef has serious optical and psychiatric problems and should seek treatment immediately.

Finally, if the planet becomes a subject with rights, it will have to be brought to trial every time an avalanche, a landslide, or a typhoon destroys not only human communities but also protected natural spaces. It matters little whether we accord an inalienable priority to human beings or the inanimate world, because it is always human beings who speak, act, and decide. We can grant horses or plane trees suffrage, but we will still be the ones who count the votes. 'I shall never say that I have a right to vote superior to that of a mosquito,' writes Arne Naess, the Norwegian founder of 'Deep Ecology'. Easy to say for a Scandinavian who has never suffered from malaria! Albert Schweitzer already said in substance that he understood that people killed mosquitoes in Africa, because of malaria, but not in Europe, where they are inoffensive. Another domain: a universal Bill of Rights for plants is available on the Internet. We have to preserve these 'extraordinary beings' who have developed a marvellous system of blooming and photosynthesis and thus 'limit the uncontrolled use of very destructive machines' such as lawnmowers, for example, and especially 'eliminate any expressions scornful of plants: scrub, weeds, undergrowth'. In 2008 a Swiss federal commission on biotechnology seriously debated the dignity and sensitivity of plants.[26] Will we soon see an anti-racist tribunal criminalizing references to the plant Sticky Willie in conversation or forbidding the use of parsley, lettuce, or endives as food on the ground that cutting them and eating them is an affront to their honour?

The argument is not untenable and it is often used, to their great indignation, against vegetarians and vegans: What do we really know about the pain felt by the vegetables we cook, the wheat we harvest, the trees we cut down? If we grant that the Earth suffers from our manoeuvres, why shouldn't plants, even if their sensations are in no way comparable to those of quadrupeds or birds? Every deep-water diver knows how algae contract at the touch of a foreign body and then spread out again. This objection, which appears ridiculous, proves that we all prosper, whether we want to or not, at the expense of vegetable, animal, or other entities, and that vegetarians are no less indifferent to the sufferings of tomatoes and beans than carnivores are to those of animals. The irony of such questions is that what we discover in this way is not the perfections of the infinitely small or of the starry sky, but rather the monstrously complex edifice of the legal sinking its claws into new objects. We may be in the middle of a conceptual recasting, but we are certainly experiencing a full-scale explosion of jargon, a proliferation of gibberish. Nature films are always odes to the beauty of the world. Activist films (*An Inconvenient Truth*, *Home*, Le *Syndrome du Titanic*), by contrast, are merely indictments of human wickedness.

To expand the sphere of the existents that have rights is simply to expand human responsibility and multiply our duties, and thus it is to plead for a broader anthropomorphism and not for a utopian ecospherism.[27] However one approaches the problem, it is always human beings who provide meaning and rights: *nature is an ethical subject only by proxy, and that is the difficulty*. In order to protect a given animal, site, or lake, we have first to deal with certain human groups. Those who scorn human exceptionalism nonetheless ceaselessly reaffirm it. The more they humble human beings, the more they distinguish them. To decree that the demarcation between the natural and the artificial is outmoded, as Hans Jonas does, to make the biped 'one citizen among others within the terrestrial community'

(Aldo Leopold), is still, under cover of humility, to invest us once again as the kings of Creation, because we alone will be judge, prosecutor, and party to the case. We think we are defending species, and everywhere we hear the echo of our own voices, we are *infinitely increasing our burden.*

Thus we are supposed to have upset 'the genesis of the weather', the orbit of the Earth, the water cycle, and the internal dynamics of nature's evolution;[28] we are also supposed to control the carbon cycle. After the Pleistocene and the Holocene, we have now entered the 'Anthropocene' (Paul Crutzen), according to the classification proposed by geologists. That is, we have entered an age in which humans construct the totality of their environment.[29] We respect the competence of scientists. Seven billion individuals now swarm over this planet, resulting in an obviously unprecedented configuration. Builders, destroyers, and profaners do not proliferate without having a strong impact on their environment. But up to what point? Putting the human species back at the centre of things – isn't that done from a philosophical point of view, prolonging Cartesianism by claiming to refute it; isn't it like rediscovering Auguste Comte's mad conviction that the human race could straighten up the Earth's axis of rotation if it wanted to?[30] Descartes at least had the prudence to declare that the human being was 'a kind of master and possessor of nature', and to emphasize by this conjunction the subaltern role of the creature. The latter could not arrogate to himself the Creator's omnipotence without offending Him; the creature was only God's delegate on Earth.

We are no longer so humble: we proclaim ourselves the captains of the ship Earth, the new princes of the world. We have hardly been toppled from our pedestal before we are put back on a still vaster throne. *Radical ecologism? It's the latest avatar of Prometheus, even if it is a penitent Prometheus.*

The Misanthrope, the Mediator, and the Militiaman

Toward the end of his life, Rousseau wrote his *Reveries of a Solitary Walker* (*Rêveries du promeneur solitaire*, 1782), a series of reflections on old age and the world. The title is misleading: Rousseau is not dreaming, and he fulminates and ruminates, he doesn't walk; he's champing at the bit, and he's never alone, always assailed by the memory of his fellows who fomented a conspiracy against him. Stretched out in his rowing boat in the middle of the Lac de Bienne in Switzerland, enjoying the pure pleasure of existing, what he still hears, behind the lapping of the waves, is the murmur of calumnies, the snigger of his enemies. 'In vain I fled into the depths of the woods, an importunate crowd followed me everywhere and veiled all of nature from my eyes.' The society of the wicked pursues him, harasses him. Paradise has to be purged of the importunate presence of people.

Less than a century later (1854), the American writer Henry David Thoreau, the inventor of the concept of civil disobedience, went off to live in solitude for two years in the woods near Concord, Massachusetts, on the banks of Walden Pond. From this experience he drew a long logbook in which praise for the 'poem of Creation' is accompanied by a critique of American society, which he saw as devoted to the god of commerce and business. A call for intensifying life by rediscovering simplicity, by turns brilliant and fastidious, the work was to have an enormous influence in the United States and marked the birth of concern about the environment (notably, it offers one of the first criticisms of eating meat). The text, torn between classical culture, oriental wisdom, and rural prosiness, is above all a meditation on the spirit of the forests, the mirror of a frozen lake, the beauty of the maple trees in the autumn. For Thoreau, the retreat to the forests elicits only one attitude: dazzled contemplation.

Between Rousseau's biliousness and the lyricism of Thoreau, who finds a certain moral purity in the trees and pastures, a third trend appears in the United States, that of the survivalists, those refractory individuals who retreat to the mountains, stock up food and medicine, have bunkers built for themselves, and learn to use weapons. They retreat in order to ward off the eventuality of a total war, plunging back into primitive life in order to prepare themselves for the worst. And sometimes they end up committing crimes, like the patriot John Pitner, who in the 1990s recruited a militia of malcontents to fight America's enemies until he was arrested by the FBI in 1997.[31] Here we find three visions that are differently modulated: nature as escape, nature as fable, nature as fortress. Today, we seem to hesitate between them: for most of those engaged in it, ecologism is a matter not of an enchanted rediscovery of landscapes and forests but rather of humanity being horrified by its image in the mirror of Creation. Our age lacks a fundamental virtue: the ability to celebrate.

5

Nature, a Cruel Stepmother or a Victim?

Article I: starting 14 July next, over the whole of the Earth's surface, days and nights will be equal in length, day will begin at 5 a.m. [. . .] Article IV: lighting and hail will never fall on forests. Humanity will be forever spared floods, and the Earth, in its full extent, will receive no more than salutary dews.

Antoine de Rivarol, parodying revolutionary decrees. *Les Actes des apôtres*, 1790

Under the love of nature, human hatred.

Marcel Gauchet, *Le Débat*, no. 60, 1990

In 1855, the American Indian chief Seattle is supposed to have written to the president of the United States:

Every part of the earth is sacred to my people. [. . .] We are part of the earth and it is part of us. [. . .] [The white man] treats his mother, the Earth, and his brother, the same, as things to be bought, pillaged, and sold like sheep or bright beads. His appetite will devour the Earth and leave behind only a desert [. . .] Man did not weave the web of life, he is merely a strand in it. Whatever he does to the web, he does to himself.[1]

Our hearts are wrung by these words: not only do they foretell the great dispossession of the Indians by the United States government, but they also resound in our ears as a warning that we do not want to hear. Thus there would be a period in the history of the human race and of nature in which humans and nature lived together in harmony? And because we have violated that alliance, we are going to pay a high price in disturbances?

On the bucolic as reconstruction

Hardly have we said farewell, in Europe at least, to the peasant world than we long for that world with its seasonal rhythms. Our wholly urban passion for the countryside comes from a melancholic perspective: nature is what is essentially lost. But these pastorals, these country idylls and fields whose sweetness we sing, are themselves fashioned by human hands. We project onto the past a purity that never existed: there was never a first morning of the world; artifice began long ago when the first farmers or nomads started to exploit their territories. According to the American biologist Edward Osborne Wilson, the massive extinction of certain animal species began in the Palaeolithic, when humans started using tools. In America, as in New Zealand, Madagascar, and Australia, humans instigated the disappearance of a major portion of the large fauna, mammals, birds, and large reptiles. Despite what Chief Seattle said, the Aborigines of Australia – like the American Indians, who are often presented as archetypes of a certain 'ecological' attitude – practised hunting by lighting fires, unhesitatingly destroying vast territories and annihilating animal species incapable of resisting them. On this level, and contrary to our sentimental vision, there is no wisdom of 'the first peoples'; they were just as brutal and destructive of their environment as we are, but were obviously less numerous.[2]

It is true that for a long time agriculture and hunting were involved in relationships of prayer and sacrifice and did not know the logic of efficiency and calculation: up to the nineteenth century, wood-cutters in Germany asked the trees to pardon them before cutting them down. What a contrast with Buffalo Bill boasting about having killed sixty-nine bison in a single day! But as soon as the first human being appeared, nature was asked to withdraw or to remain within quotation marks. The beautiful countryside that we celebrate is an artifice, as was already the forest in Heidegger or, in our own time, the North American 'wilderness', which is primitive and protective at once. The dream of a peasant Arcadia, of a lost Eden that could provide for everyone's needs without exception, is a retrospective projection. The state of nature is an invention of Progress. If, as Goethe said, it is now for urbanites 'the great tranquillizer of the modern soul', that is because it incarnates a harmony that contrasts with the chaos of our metropolises. In the re-created rural world that is our own, city-dwellers seek a haven of peace, a brief suspension of worries and hardships: there, no one provokes them or assails their integrity. In countrysides domesticated by centuries of agriculture, I relax, recuperate, remain 'entwined with myself' (Rousseau).

Thus in the modern period, rural life became the paradigm of health, of the idyll, and of moderation. To challenge that norm, to violate its majesty, is potentially to put the whole cosmic edifice in danger. It is the Planet, the great victim of human history, that has to be protected, Michel Serres tells us, just as the Declaration of the Rights of Man protected slaves and outcasts.[3] But to advocate this kind of 'natural contract' on the basis of reciprocity and symbiosis is at least to suppose that our power is as great as Gaia's. There's the rub: first we are told that humans are all-powerful, the instigators of all kinds of general problems, and then they are put back in their place by an entity furious at having been subjected to violence. We are either children to be scolded or strapping youths taking our Mother Earth in our arms.[4] So we become the mothers of our moribund Mother![5] Jonas already suggested that we see the world as a mother giving her baby tender care: loving power yielding to absolute weakness. A moving image, but one whose empirical counterpart is not easily found. We have seen how ecological discourse constantly wavers between megalomania and humility without being able to choose between these two options.

Science made a great step forward when the notion of sympathy was rejected as a precondition of knowledge and analogical thought was abandoned as a superstition. To see in the behaviour of animals, plants, and the planets a moral correspondence with the behaviour of human beings is to make it impossible to understand their own laws. We had to go beyond what our senses can perceive, and science is only 'a series of errors refuted' (Bachelard). This meant the end of the ancient cosmos that imposed its laws on everything that existed on Earth and in the heavens.[6] So we had to distance ourselves from nature, objectify it, and substitute a more neutral taxonomy for anthropocentric classifications. But what scientists separated (thus giving birth to disciplines as diverse as chemistry, botany, geology, and astrophysics), a new sensibility that has grown up since the Enlightenment and Romanticism has sought to unite again, offering the promise of a reconciliation between humans and the living. A poetics of the elements of fire, water, air, and earth (Bachelard) thus redoubles the repulsion science shows with regard to an affective approach to phenomena.

Thus we return to the Platonic idea of a soul that acts universally in each of the animate species and grants animals a kind of immortality. Animals are our brothers because they suffer and take pleasure just as we do. They will be resurrected on Judgment Day, along with lice, spiders, and toads, and will cease to moan once the malediction of Original Sin has been lifted.[7] Whereas the pioneers of the scientific spirit extolled distance, poets and philanthropists advocate friendship and the rules of a cordial imagination. No doubt animals, plants, and mountain ranges have their own laws, but they are also our reflection, part of our presence scattered over the universe. They are in us, just as we are in them. We no longer understand why in Britain, up to the nineteenth century, cutting down oak trees was seen as a contribution to Progress[8] and a way of managing 'barbarism', whereas we attribute a quasi-sacred character to trees such as sycamores and beeches. A little of us dies when we destroy them. In moments of communion with a magnificent panorama, we experience a solidarity with living beings united by a single envelope, a single tunic. The Utopian Charles Fourier proposed that the Milky Way, which is the luminous projection of human seminal activity, be multiplied by accelerating sexual unions. Thus the problem of lighting large cities at night would be solved if only men and women copulated constantly and in every way possible. (This is a project that should be immediately put before the secretary-general of the United Nations.) Fourier also imagined that in his New World the most recalcitrant species would be put at the service of all, thanks to 'the brilliant products of the new creation', so that antiwhales would draw vessels into calmer waters in the event of a storm, while anti-crocodiles ('river co-operators') and anti-seals (sea-horses) would provide rapid transportation.

Zoophilia, theoretical and practical

We no longer believe that creation is put at the service of human beings in order to entertain or feed us; we no

longer inflict capital punishment on horses, bears, or
pigs that are guilty of homicides.[9] We no longer believe
that animality haunts insane asylums, the poor, savages,
or beggars. We rightly punish any manifestation of
cruelty toward our 'inferior brothers'. We now seek to
bridge the gap that separates us from animals, to find
out whether they are moved by instinct or reason,
capable of being trained, or even if they might someday,
like certain great apes, learn to speak and put together
a hundred or two hundred words. We share with them
a community of fate; their joy delights us, their pain
dismays us. Constantly exploited, beaten, and hunted
as an inexhaustible resource, the animal used to be at
the same time valued and advocated as a companion.
The exploitation of many species is compensated by
privileging a few others with which we enter into dialogue and with which we live. We have attached to our
lives cats, dogs, canaries, finches, horses, and so on
(whose excretions are a serious problem in urban areas),
which we often treat better than human beings. For
instance, the obsession with dogs among the English
aristocracy, which is keen on hunting and deeply concerned about pedigree, and the slow promotion of cats
since the Middle Ages, when they were initially dispar-
aged as Satanic and then brought into the sphere of the
family as household gods, typify this elevation of a few
species to the detriment of others. The infatuation with
felines and their nonchalant beauty and the taste for
aviaries or exotic animals is a matter of sentimentality
and aesthetics. This selective zoolatry, the immoderate
love for a Siamese, a bulldog, or a stallion, sometimes
degenerates into misanthropy, and is not incompatible
with an extraordinary ferocity with regard to other
animals. Quadrupeds and birds will always have the
advantage over our human brothers and sisters that they
do not talk back and seem, through their muteness, to
acquiesce to everything we say. Schopenhauer, a great

misanthrope *sub specie aeternitatis* and the founder of
the Society for the Protection of Animals in Frankfurt,
adored his poodle. When the dog exasperated him, he
called it a human.

A people's domestic pets tell us a great deal about its
mentality. There will always be eccentrics who keep
animals that common sense rejects, such as rats, vermin,
snakes, tarantulas, and crows. There are no easy, serene
relationships with animals, only whims, repulsions. For
the past century we have been going through a fascinating redefinition of the boundary lines separating humans
from animals, the wild from the domestic. A whole
buried tradition stretching from Ovid to Saint Francis
of Assisi has been exhumed and re-examined. A body
of thought is developing among ethologists, neurolo-
gists, and philosophers that redraws the old lines of
separation. Perfectibility is conferred, within certain
limits, on animals as well; they can tip into a certain
kind of humanization just as humans can slip into
animality.

However, we are far from the reconciliation promised
by the Gospels. This great blurring of the boundaries
does not mean that harmony will reign, that the hunter
will have a drink with the wolf, or that we will cease to
eat meat or to domesticate and exploit certain species.
The relationships will be marked by conflicts, excesses,
and immoderate love and indifference.

It is said that when a parrot belonging to Henry VIII
fell into the Thames, it squawked 'A boat! A boat!
twenty pounds for a boat!'[10] But after a sailor fished it
out of the water and brought it to the king, the bird
changed its tone and said: 'Give the knave a groat.'
What is it that we find fascinating about certain animals?
Such a distance within such a nearness. Rousseau saw
orang-utans as a species of humans the brevity of whose
lives had prevented them from developing their faculties. From Victor, the eighteenth-century wild child of

the Aveyron whom hunters had found naked and hirsute, to our cats and dogs that are so 'civilized' that they suffer from depression, go to the hairdresser, the perfumer, the pedicurist, and even the psychologist, we are constantly changing our prerogatives. We know that certain canines die of sorrow on the graves of the masters. Humans can be raised selectively, just like horses and cattle, and animals are now used therapeutically to relieve the anxiety of the ill, notably in retirement homes.

The fact that our species and others are intertwined does not make them more transparent. On the contrary. *To note the numerous resemblances is also to acknowledge that there is an unbridgeable gulf.* Someone who tries to act like an angel is acting like an animal, Pascal said. But trying to act like an animal is hopelessly human. We are not just animals, and that's the whole problem. What connects us with the great apes does not cover everything we are. This minuscule gap cannot be crossed. We are primates plus a certain something that makes us human.[11] This does not prevent us, however, from talking on and on to each other in a marvellous dialogue of the deaf. We pretend to converse with our furry and feathered companions, and they have the delicacy to feign approbation. On the basis of this great misunderstanding, the most harmonious relationships flourish (that is more or less the definition of a happy marriage). The long soliloquy of a lady walking her dog while talking to it may not be absurd for her or for him. She cuddles him, reassures him; it's a kind of music that they play together.

This new distribution of roles occasionally goes haywire: to the will to renaturalize human beings, who are seen as guilty of having freed themselves from their essence, corresponds, among some vegetarians, the temptation to denature wild animals, to re-educate carnivores, to teach Rottweilers, foxes, jaguars, and jackals the joys of eating fruit and berries. These missionaries

for human rights in the animal domain have long years
of work ahead of them! Let us also mention the more
or less demoniacal projects in the style of Doctor
Moreau, the hero of H.G. Wells's eponymous novel
(1896), a mad scientist of vivisection who has created,
on a distant island, a race of artificial beings, half-
human, half-animal, and is killed by one of his rebel-
lious creatures, a human–puma hybrid. Still more:
philosophers of animal ethics like Peter Singer advocate
engaging in 'heavy petting' with one's dog or even one's
horse, cow, goat, or ass. With a straight face, Singer sets
out to analyse the notion of amorous caresses with a
tomcat or a lapdog.[12] Bestiality is just one taboo among
others, and history offers many examples of it, especially in rural areas, where the strictly guarded morality
of girls allowed hardly any outlet for the sexual drives
of boys, who relieved themselves with cows and mares.
Can one French kiss one's dog, or fondle one's sow?
Does one have the right, the eminent professor asks, to
have oneself fellated by a young calf used to nursing on
its mother, and isn't sodomizing a hen or a duck, a cruel
act that usually ends with the hen's death, ultimately a
less serious offence than raising it in a battery where it
would be killed in any case? We should not be shocked
to find ourselves desired by apes or when a dog comes
to rub its penis on our leg. We are animals like them,[13]
subject to the same drives. There is nothing wrong
about different species giving each other pleasure, Singer
assures us. Apart from the perplexity that it may arouse,
Singer's text raises at least two questions. The first is
that of the carnal obsession that already runs through
relations between men and women: can one love one's
dog without engaging in sex with it? The second is
moral: must we court animals and win their consent
before we touch them? Will there someday be law firms
specializing in the sexual harassment of animals? Who
will file the complaint? Magnificent legal battles can be
foreseen.

The annexation to the domestic sphere of a few furry or feathered specimens appears to broaden the domain of our peers. But by choosing a pony, a puss, or a Labrador as a quasi-brother, this similarity is shifted toward a surprising otherness. Thinking we are anthropomorphizing our inferior brothers, we in fact make ourselves more like them. We try to teach them our language but we also try to acquire the instinct and sense of smell that characterizes them and that we have lost. This is the case for 'echolocation', a faculty peculiar to bats or dolphins that is developed by some blind people, and consists in 'visualizing' the environment in three dimensions by interpreting echoes bouncing back from surrounding objects. What is specific to human beings is that we don't know who we are, that we always exceed our definition: thinking we are extending our domain, we decline into plants, trees, cetaceans, winning back faculties lost by walking erect and civilization. This new sharing of sovereignty, this great redistricting, thus signifies a new question about ourselves: 'If there were no animals, human nature would be even more incomprehensible' (Buffon).

Nature is not our guide

Ecology has a choice between two directions: declaring anti-humanism as its principle, celebrating rivers and forests the better to castigate human beings, or adopting an open anthropocentrism that embraces humanity, nature, and animals in a general good will, so that no category suffers pointless harm. The Old Testament and the Church Fathers emphasized how much malice toward our inferior brothers hardens our hearts against our human brothers. 'Love God, love His creatures,' said priests and pastors. People who brutalize asses, horses, oxen, dogs, or cats will someday end up brutalizing other humans: Claude Lévi-Strauss adopted this argument term for term. A fascinating contradiction: it is within the ancient anthropocentric tradition that a new attitude of respect for other species emerged.[14] Thus there are two kinds of humanism: one lends its voice to the Earth, like a ventriloquist, in order to oppose human beings; the other argues in favour of a new approach to nature and the human species taken together. Saving nature is also a way of saving ourselves.

Why try to save the remaining populations of tigers or rhinoceroses, why lament the deforestation of whole sections of Brazil or Borneo? Out of sentimentalism, because 'everything that lives is holy' (William Blake), each shrub sacred, each blade of grass divine? No doubt. But especially in order to preserve a wealth without which our humanity would feel diminished, to protect the multiple faces of Creation in its marvellous prodigality. A devastated world would mark not the triumph but the devastation of the human itself. The value of the Komodo dragon, the Florida puma, or the bearded vulture consists in their profound gratuitousness. Even if they protect ecosystems in their own way, they 'serve' no purpose in the utilitarian sense of the term, and that is why they are precious to us. They manifest the baroque exuberance of the living, which proliferates its creations in every direction. It is in fact toward the broadening of the sense of humanity and of our duties that we must work, and not toward a narrowing of the human being, whose responsibility now extends to a domain wider than his or her simple praxis. Thus we are compelled to become 'planetary physicians', to use Lovelock's expression, that is, our own physicians, but with limited competence, because in caring for the environment, we are contributing to our own fulfilment. To recognize a crime against humanity's heritage is first of all to fight on our own behalf.

But this will to respect our habitat must not lead us into an idolatry of nature. For example, Hans Jonas, reproducing the ancient vision of the cosmos as the structure and model of the social and individual order, explained that the supreme ends reside in nature. Thus in his view, technology is guilty of a twofold crime: destroying the environment and modifying the boundary between the living and the non-living, if need be by substituting itself for the living. For Jonas, robotics and cloning are threats as grave as the possible annihilation of the world by nuclear weapons, and they are terrifying because they seek to improve human beings, to 'augment' them, as the current terminology puts it. What frightens this father of ecologism is not the risk of the worst happening; it is 'the menace of the best', to borrow Étienne Barillier's formulation.[15] Here we touch upon the true project of a radical ecologism: to condemn humans for having revolted against their fate in order to improve their condition. Gaia is thus supposed to be the counter-model that will be used to put the impudent creature back in its place. Everywhere, our nourishing Mother vetoes our deviations and commands us to stop everything on pain of reprisals. As for the nature that we encounter all around us, it continues to outwit us on the physical, climatic, and geological levels. It is neither good nor bad; it is indifferent: it is waging a pitiless war against us, it programmes us to live, but also to die; it offers us the brightest outlook, subjects us to the worst tortures, shows itself to be both marvellous and abject. In no case could it constitute our code of behaviour, a guide for action. The whole human adventure is a merciless struggle against the physical, biological, and psychological fatalities imposed on our species. Should we sign 'a pact of courtesy' with the elements, as Michel Serres demands? Just try courtesy in dealing with a tsunami, a tornado! *We have to protect nature, but we also have to protect ourselves against nature.*

After the End of the World

In a Buddhist monastery in Tibet, tucked away more than 5,000 metres above sea level, monks recite day and night the nine billion versions of the name of God, each containing at least nine characters. According to a legend, when this exercise is completed, life on Earth will end. Two monks who have heard about an extraordinary machine, the computer, ask their superiors for permission to go to buy one over there, in faraway America. After travelling for a month, they arrive in the United States, and return with an enormous device carried by human bearers. Two American technicians, non-believers, accompany them to programme the machine. It begins to digest the list of names at a speed that stupefies the monks. After months of operation, the names of God are exhausted. The Americans flee the monastery, fearing the believers' wrath when they note the failure of the prediction. As they escape toward the valley under cover of night, they turn around: in the Himalayan sky, the stars are going out one by one; the disc of the moon is fading away . . .

This story by Arthur C. Clarke, written in 1954, is marvellous in that it puts the most advanced science in the service of the most superstitious belief. What if it were true, if it sufficed to recite the names of God to put an end to things? The theme of the end of the world has a double connotation, messianic and punitive. In one case, it is a matter of creating a break in human time to rescue humans and favour their accession to the Kingdom of God: in the year 1,000 the seas will overflow, mountains will collapse, armies of demons will sow discord, and Christ will return to save the Just. In the other case, it is a matter of punishing humans for their audacity: science and industry have seriously damaged our living space. According to its detractors, the experiment begun in the sixteenth century under the aegis of reason and happiness will end in chaos. In the spring of 2011, Nobel Prize winners constituted themselves as a tribunal to judge and rebuke humanity. By trying to free humans from Original Sin, modern times have broadened the scope of the prosecution to History as a whole. But David M. Raup, a palaeontologist, tells us that even if we were to blow up our whole nuclear arsenal, thus provoking the interruption of photosynthesis and the elimination of the human race, the biosphere would not disappear and bacterial life would continue, hardly affected, just as it did after giant meteorites hit the Earth. 'We are virtually powerless over the earth at our planet's own geological timescale' (Stephen Jay Gould).[16] A little puzzle: if you were going to die tomorrow in a nuclear attack, what would you do? Essentially: make love with your beloved or with others, to the point of satiety, enjoy a gigantic feast with all possible excesses, because it wouldn't matter any more. Even in the worst episodes – wars, genocides – there are always those who escape, showing the species' extraordinary resistance, emerging from the ruins and charnel houses and beginning the human adventure all over again. They are mutants, like the people already depicted in Cormac McCarthy's novel *The Road*, post-mortem living beings who move through a landscape of ashes from which vegetation and animals have disappeared. At the end of the horror, there is still a possibility for humans.

It is never the end of the world, it is always the end of a world.

6

Science in the Age of Suspicion

Man has risen or declined (however you want to see it) from the King of Creation he thought himself to the role of the holder of a franchise on a planet.

Antoine Augustin Cournot, French mathematician, 1872

The 'certainties' characteristic of scientific knowledge are not all 'equally certain', and there is nothing to indicate that we are getting closer to [. . .] that final fusion of Immovable Knowledge with Irresistible Ignorance.

Stanislaw Lem, 'The World as Cataclysm', 1986

Around the deathbed of Madame Bovary, who has poisoned herself, two irreconcilable enemies talk as they watch over her body: the Abbé Bournisien, an ignorant, sanctimonious, and sectarian priest, and the pharmacist Homais, a resolute Voltairean, freethinker, and heir of the Enlightenment who violently rejects the Church and its superstitions. In his view, only science can break the hold of prejudices and emancipate humans from biblical fables by making them free. In this dialogue, Flaubert's genius consists not in taking sides in favour of the cleric or the apothecary: he shows, in this nocturnal confrontation of characters, the core of a twofold stupidity, religious and scientistic. What is striking in the remarks they exchange is their similarity: the abbé and the pharmacist are both reciting a catechism. Science has fought religion only to become a religion in turn. Here Flaubert draws up a typology of false adversaries: two persons can argue implacably with one another while remaining utterly identical. In the wee hours of the morning, Bournisien and Homais, brought together by their mutual hunger, begin to drink, and eat a hearty breakfast, admitting, 'We shall end by understanding one another.'

In our own time we could imagine a third figure alongside this legendary couple, one that would have something of both the others: that of the scientist who renounces science out of fear of its devastating effects, as Einstein regretted having encouraged President Roosevelt to produce the atomic bomb, and later became an opponent of nuclear weapons. Here we no longer have the priest castigating human folly, but the sorcerer's apprentice rejecting his inventions. The Saviour has become the Killer: making discoveries used to be his grandeur; now his wisdom consists in repenting. The intoxication of unveiling is replaced by the passion for disavowal.

The universe of evil spells

Science is in the position of the accused: it has changed the world but it has not cured it. It has done away with so many evils that we have forgotten them, but it has added new ones for which we reproach it. It promised us the emancipation of humanity; now we want to be emancipated from the emancipator. We are indeed the heirs of Louis Pasteur and of Frankenstein, of mad hope combined with unlimited dread. The medical errors committed in France and in Europe over the past two decades – growth hormones, Vioxx, the contaminated blood scandal, and, more recently, Benfluorex – have contributed not a little to this distrust. What is going on here? The thing that is supposed to cure us can also kill us. This coincidence of the drug that heals and a poison, even though it was emphasized by Plato under the name of *pharmakon*, is intolerable for us. When a single brand, a single drug, reveals its harmfulness, the whole chain of pharmaceutical vigilance is contaminated: the agent of our health becomes the agent of our destruction. Progress multiplies the factors of uncertainty: thus feeding ourselves, caring for ourselves, and moving about all become as delicate as crossing a minefield. The whole technological universe rebels against us like an army of malicious spirits determined to cut us to pieces. A terrible danger lurks under the appearances of everyday life:

> The world of the visible must be investigated, relativized and evaluated with respect to a second reality, only existent in thought and not concealed in the world. [. . .] Dangerous, hostile substances lie concealed behind the harmless façades. [. . .] Those who simply use things, take them as they appear, who only breathe and eat, without an inquiry into the background toxic reality, are not only naïve but they also misunderstand the hazards that threaten them, and thus expose themselves to such hazards with no protection. Abandonment, direct enjoyment, simple being-so are broken. Everywhere, pollutants and toxins laugh and play their tricks like devils in the Middle Ages.[1]

Even if technological accidents have caused relatively few victims (12,000 dead in Bhopal, India, in 1984 after an explosion at a Union Carbide chemical plant, thirty dead in Toulouse in 2001 after an accident at another chemical plant), their symbolic impact is devastating. These figures are minimal in comparison to the twenty

million deaths in the Spanish flu epidemic of 1918 or
the 500,000 deaths caused by the cyclone in the Bhola
district of Bangladesh in 1970; but the number doesn't
matter. These events were caused by humans, and
thus they constitute a broken promise of which medicine and chemistry, those industries of well-being, are
guilty. Imagine your child hospitalized for a simple
appendicitis and plunged into a coma after contracting
a nosocomial infection (that is, one contracted in the
hospital; in France, there are 4,200 such cases every
year). What is broken then is the blind faith that allows
us to entrust ourselves to a specialist the way people
used to entrust themselves to their priests. The treatment for a problem has itself become another problem.
Scientists want to do us good but end up harming us
without knowing it.

Thus science has lost its arrogance: it is no longer the
block of prodigious discoveries that dazzled Jules Verne
and Victor Hugo and that bordered on the sublime, and
it is still less the royal road to Eden that Francis Bacon
saw in it in the seventeenth century. The myth of the
mad scientist prey to his dominating impulses, from
Mabuse to Mengele, has supplanted the generous good-
ness of a Pasteur or a Schweitzer. A person whose power
invests him with an excessive power wants to enslave
humanity to further his criminal designs. He becomes a
diploma-holding annex to the dictator and often his
ally, and concentrates in his hands an unheard-of power.
After Hiroshima, Chernobyl, and Fukushima, serenity
no longer seems possible. The whole framework of
everyday life is subject to examination, beginning with
our food. Eating has become an act almost as perilous
as bungee-jumping: 'Eating kills' was the headline
(meant seriously) in the French magazine *Télérama*
(March 2011), a lapidary statement that no anorexic
would deny but which will puzzle starving people in the
Sahel. Our ancestors suffered from hunger; we suffer

from indigestion. 'The time has already come when at
mealtimes, instead of wishing each other *bon appétit,*
we would be better off wishing each other good luck,'
writes Pierre Rabhi, an apostle of organic agriculture.
An avalanche of poisonous products has been introduced into our fruits and vegetables, pesticides and
other substances that destroy our appetites. Every
mouthful is a potential cancer that we are inviting into
our bodies. As for meat, it is not only harmful but
criminal, and its production leads to intensive deforestation, ruined soils, erosion, the impoverishment of
agricultures, an excessive waste of energy, and the maintenance of hundreds of millions of livestock whose
intestinal gases contribute to the greenhouse effect.[2]
People who eat meat are dupes twice over: accomplices
of sanguinary animal factories and terrible hen-battery
operations, they also collaborate in their own destruction by ingesting steaks or chickens with contaminated
flesh. Vegetarianism has become a literary genre in its
own right, divided into several hostile and competing
sects.[3] Let us recall that in many cultures, the trades
practised by butchers and executioners are taboo; in
France, in June 2011, butchers rightly protested the use
of the expression 'the butcher of the Balkans' to describe
General Mladic, who had been arrested in Belgrade for
crimes of genocide.

But the malediction extends even to vegetables, as
was shown in spring 2011 by the affair of the 'killer
cucumber' in Germany, which gave rise to a veritable
abdication of the understanding in that country and
provoked a crisis that is said to have cost Europe almost
500 million euros. The German federal authorities
began by accusing produce from Spain before recognizing that the lethal bacteria came from germinated seeds
used in organic farming (other contaminations with the
E. coli bacteria struck in Lille and Bordeaux). In theory,
the organic label is supposed to eliminate doubt; but

doubt returned with unprecedented force as soon as it was offered the slightest opportunity. This indictment of the vegetable, which had up to that point been endowed with all the virtues, is a symbolic tragedy: henceforth no industry is immune to suspicion. Now the vegetable, that sacred fruit from Gaia's womb, that vehicle of redemption, is betraying us as well! In rejecting phytosanitary products and by using natural fertilizers such as manure, organic farming is potentially just as harmful as industrial agriculture (but we have not heard its proponents' *mea culpa*). There is no sanctuary; we are surrounded. Watermelons, squash, potatoes, and cherries can also turn into monsters. (Here again cinema anticipated reality in a very funny, very bad 1978 film by John De Bello called *The Attack of the Killer Tomatoes*; it is a parody of *Jaws* in which apparently harmless tomatoes attack swimmers, assault cooks, and transform peaceful America into torrents of ketchup.)

Food poses a twofold problem: ethical and dietetic. We have to ensure that its producers have been paid a fair price and that animals have not been subjected to cruel or degrading treatment. Then we have to check whether it presents any major risk to our health. Eating is a craft in itself that involves calculating calories, industrial espionage, the detection of evil spirits, and discussion forums. That soup heating on the stove, the delicious stew simmering there, are veritable Seveso sites, little chemical factories that you are about to ingest in all innocence. The dice are loaded: agro-alimentary firms and multinationals have been conspiring for half a century to poison us with our consent. Carbonated drinks given women increase their chances of delivering babies before term; saccharine and cyclamates increase the risk of cancer; as for additives and colorants, they kill us insidiously. There is no longer any product, from bread to tea, that escapes suspicion. In the old days, we were protected by a veil of ignorance.

But the more we know, the more we suffer. Knowledge progresses to the detriment of insouciance.

The spirit of investigation sometimes destroys itself by excess. Consider, for example, this result reported in a study that appeared on 1 December 2010: 'In a single day, a ten-year-old child's food is likely to expose him to 128 chemical residues proceeding from 81 different substances. Forty-two of these substances are classified as "possible or probable carcinogens," and five as "proven carcinogens". Thirty-seven substances also disturb the endocrine glands.'[4] One wonders how, after such a deluge, our children don't emerge from the cafeteria looking like the Elephant Man or the Hunchback of Notre Dame. As for flavour and the art of living represented by good dining, they are in danger of becoming the first victims of this hygienic obsession. The sense of a noble product is being effaced by the concern for a healthy product. The taste of exquisite dishes, the transmission of recipes, the pleasure of sharing good things, constantly struggle with the fear of digging our own graves with our teeth. In this respect, restaurants serving organic food are less places of delight than temples of regeneration: in them we are attending mass, we chew assiduously, and see ourselves as escapees from the great industrial system. We drink our nettle juice, eat our Jerusalem artichoke soup, and sip our herbal tea with all the gravity of high priests. Alimentary rituals formerly prescribed by religion or tradition are now governed by anxiety concerning our chances of surviving our meals. It is no longer the scantiness but the abundance of our food that is involved. We forget that in rich countries, and especially in North America, it is the enormity of the portions, starting with breakfast, that is in question for a civilization of plethora that mass-produces obesity. Everywhere the concern about quality has to wrestle with the obsession about quantity, which is never merely a fear of not having enough.

The imaginary doctor

Since Molière and Jules Romains's Dr Knock, we know that medical knowledge can make us sick. Now that we have iatrogenic infections and dangerous drugs, we know that it can also kill us. How foolish we were to believe in the curative virtues of our remedies: aspirin and paracetamol can make our sons sterile and hasten our daughters' arrival at puberty. Strange names – 'phtalate', 'paraben' – enter into our everyday vocabulary. We are becoming apothecaries hunched over our files, warily considering the products that have been prescribed for us. No potion or gelcap is swallowed without a careful examination of its undesirable side-effects, the list of which is dizzyingly long. The antidote seems more dangerous than the affliction. We judge everything in complete ignorance, but every investigation published in the newspapers or on the Web contradicts earlier ones, increasing our perplexity. The household pharmaceutical budget is exploding: our medicine cabinets overflow with unused vials, pills, and syrups that will end up in the rubbish bin. The sick wants to be their own doctors, and display the mad erudition of incompetents: they combine an acute knowledge of points of detail with a bottomless ignorance of the essential. The more medical science treats us, the more it increases our anxiety. From snoring to sexual potency to acne, everything becomes a source of worry: even fellatio and cunnilingus are suspected of spreading cancer, the papillomavirus. Sexual pleasure is no longer compatible with health. A hard time for hypochondriacs, who are now beaten on their own terrain by a society that never ceases to tell them: you are right to be concerned. Worry yourself sick! Doubt feeds on the means that are advanced to challenge it. Every day new diseases are invented, and who would dare to say that they are well?

The disappearance of religion, in Europe at least, is a matter not of the disenchantment of the world, but instead of the return of the supernatural, everywhere, including in technological objects. The fantastic bestiary of the *Ancien Régime*, with its succubi, ghosts, vampires, and werewolves, has been reincarnated in these conveniences that are supposed to serve us. The apparently most anodyne – mobile phones, Christmas toys, relay antennas – are bearers of spells. Some disturb our endocrine systems, others are allergenic or spread cancer. Since suspicion is a contagious disease, the solutions for the problem are themselves the bearers of pernicious effects. Take low-consumption light bulbs: in addition to the fact that they don't produce light, they contain mercury, which is very bad if it is released into the environment. As for the much-vaunted wind turbines, they produce about as much noise as a railway switching yard, as well as tinnitus and pressure on the eardrums. Their reflective blades dazzle walkers and their immense structures cause a specific kind of vertigo. They are also said to cause sleep disturbances, cardiac arrhythmias, and headaches, and to disturb livestock and pets for two kilometres around.[5] Their blades are alleged to kill bats, decimating a species that plays the role of a natural insecticide. Alternative medicines, with their cortege of essential oils, cloves, and valerian, can be dangerous; certain plants, even in small doses, are genuine poisons. Our efforts to correct the damage done by progress give rise in turn to new calamities. We are passing not from something bad to something better but from one problem to another. To progress is to change to a different form of servitude, to throw off one chain in order to put on another. Thus we move in a world of omens, demoniacal forces that have to be flushed out. The precautionary principle, which was written into the French constitution after the contaminated blood scandal, has not attenuated this dramatization, because it has become the principle of suspicion and especially the principle of conspiracy. It does not function 'as a complication of scientific decisions, but rather as a gradual disqualification of science in decision-making'.[6] From a semantic point of view, taking precautions means (in French, at least) telling children to go to the toilet before leaving on a trip. The Greek term *phronesis* ('prudence'), the art of conducting oneself in an uncertain matter, seems more appropriate for collective action. The desire to eliminate all uncertainty is increased by the impossibility of doing so, and degenerates into an aversion to risk. The demand for security is insatiable and feeds a continually expanding market that ranges from doctors to insurance by way of courts and auditors: the psychologist, the judge, and the expert witness form an implacable trio required to register our complaints, to calm our fears. This desire for protection multiplies imaginary dangers: everything becomes a peril, an abyss, a fall. To live, simply to live, is too costly an experience. The technological, medial, and alimentary edifice has taken on the appearance of a monstrous fatality. Paul Virilio points out that 'to invent the railway train is to invent derailing, and to invent electricity is also to invent electrocution'.[7] In the same vein, we might add that to invent rope is to invent hanging, and to invent the needle is to invent the prick. There comes a time when it is philosophers themselves, prey to their manias, who go off the rails.

The panic of reason

Science, a school of probity and rigour, thus loses its moral magisterium. In Europe, it has been deserted by many students, who prefer more profitable programmes of study such as law and finance. The triumph of greed and the culture of lawsuits are eating away, like a kind of leprosy, at the whole edifice of our societies, especially in the United States. They inhibit innovation

– unless we consider the crazy algorithms constructed by brokers to diversify debts to be a type of progress – and give rise to a profusion of parasitical professions: barristers, solicitors, traders.[8] We no longer want to rely on science to guide us because it has lost, for the time being, its rationality credit.[9] Two attitudes will be demanded of it: pedagogy and self-criticism. Let it condemn its errors, practise humility, multiply intelligent popularizations, and bring people up to date on all the most difficult kinds of knowledge.

Even when informed, the ordinary citizen is incapable of apprehending the whole of a discipline or of forming an opinion about precise points in physics or biotechnology. To put science under surveillance is not necessarily to endow it with a conscience; it is to add to its complex procedures a meddling that might remind us of the obscurantism of the Cultural Revolution in China or of the Khmer Rouge. Scientists, biologists, or researchers have perhaps lost their authority, but the eminence dissipated in this way has been transferred to those who pride themselves on their status and make decisions about everything or nothing. How can one determine the advisability of constructing a pressurized water reactor if one is not oneself a specialist in nuclear physics capable of debating the subject with one's peers? And yet democracy demands that we make decisions, with due understanding, once we are enlightened and informed. In surgery, for instance, doctors can explain to us all the possible options, but they do not relieve us of the obligation of taking a risk. Thus patients, without real knowledge and basing themselves on the assurances of their medical team, have to make a decision regarding what they hope will be the least dangerous solution. In other words, science and technology are first of all acts of faith, and at present we are going through a very serious crisis in this regard.

At one time or another, every discipline has to retranslate its symbolic system into a language accessible to a lay audience, and avoid jargon. But this simple discourse also requires a level of competence that is not accessible to everyone. For example, on what basis could we reject an invention in the agricultural domain? In the name of the competence of the farmer, cattleman, winemaker, or that of the feeling of the random citizen who decides every question? This is all the ambiguity of the 'deliberative forums' that are supposed to create fair rules to establish common life. What legitimacy should be accorded to groups of activists, NGOs, or neighbours who act because they fear potential damage? The Treaty of Lisbon signed in 2006 introduced a new procedure, the 'European Citizens' Initiative', which is supposed to allow any petition signed by at least one million persons from the European Union to initiate new legal actions. How can we guarantee that this interventionism will not be the spearhead of a militant ignorance in which people will brandish their political convictions and sufferings in order to censure the slightest proposal? Before deliberating on genetic engineering, robotics, or nanotechnologies, one has to understand, become a listener, a student. Unless one allows the deliberation to be conducted by official experts, who are often consultants for large firms, or to activists, who generally combine a very partial knowledge with an absolute intolerance: in France, consider the example of the volunteers who destroyed genetically modified grapevines under the guidance of the extreme-left nationalist José Bové.[10]

To expand the circle of expertise to the NGOs that have suddenly become decision-makers in environmental politics, over and above representative institutions, is especially to expand the circle of the arbitrary. Moreover, what is the basis of these large associations' legitimacy? In the name of what do they speak? Who mandates them, who pays them, what are their methods? Who will investigate the WWF, Oxfam, Greenpeace, or Friends of the Earth the way Monsanto, Total, or BP are investigated? In the contemporary imagination, the multinationals are the equivalent of totalitarian states: cold monsters, indifferent to human lives, prepared to do anything in order to prosper. That is what makes the debate on nuclear power so abstruse: the arrogance of the technocrats and nuclear lobbies finds its counterpart in the vituperations of their adversaries. A double dead end that leaves ordinary citizens unsatisfied, as if they had been the dupes of a twofold misunderstanding. Large firms can be demonized, but their expertise can also be used, they can be restrained by concrete commitments, and it is possible to cooperate with them, as do some NGOs, in order to help them avoid fatal mistakes. After all, a company's self-interest commands it to be respectful of the environment and accepted by the people. In a strictly economic logic, every incident is very expensive, in terms of image and finances, and it can be fatal, even to a large group (Union Carbide almost disappeared after Bhopal, and BP was seriously affected by the oil spill in the Gulf of Mexico in 2009).

The world changes more rapidly than our capacities for understanding it. Scientists themselves know nothing about their colleagues' very narrow specialities. That is the whole difficulty of a 'citizens' science' in which an attempt is made to associate the general public with the most recent discoveries. What happens when the general public wants to move from the status of listener to that of 'supervisor of decisions' or even 'co-legislator'?[11] No matter how much we know, it will always be too little, especially when a decision has to be made in favour of new sources of energy: shale gas or third- or fourth-generation reactors. It is always a matter of making a decision in half-darkness because by nature science produces unknowns. We have to undertake vast national consultations on crucial topics, but it is an illusion to think that they will magically resolve all our problems. No one escapes the unforeseeable, not even abstentionists: for example, how can we know whether in a context of decreasing agricultural yields throughout the world, the prohibition of GMOs might not ultimately be a criminal act that would condemn whole countries to malnutrition? The prohibition of DDT as a result of pressure applied in the 1970s by environmental groups in rich countries led to new outbreaks of malaria in the South, that is, to millions of deaths, even if the controversy over the harmfulness of this insecticide is still going on. Avoidance can do just as much harm as use: the 'precautionists' would like to barricade themselves in an irreproachable position. But such an attitude is no more secure than the other. There comes a time when we have to decide, leap into the unknown: no prudence can eliminate this element of the aleatory, which is inseparable from making a decision.

On the ground that not everything that is possible in matters of science is desirable, must we staunch all possibilities and close the door to the slightest innovations? We are living amid full-blown 'epistemophobia', as Dominique Lecourt very aptly calls it.[12] While technological objects stimulate nature, modify it, and substitute themselves for it by fabricating living beings, as in the case of genetic engineering, a veritable panic is born from a possible confusion of orders. Just as a computer virus copies the operation of a biological virus by infecting software programs, the fantasies of aliens or cyborgs that combine a brain and a computer surge up again with every innovation. The hybrid creature, a mixture of human and animal, of human and machine (*Terminator*, *Robocop*, *Matrix*), or of reptile and pathogenic germs embodies, in a way, the worst characteristics of all species: the animal's instinct, human beings' cruelty, and the implacable automatism of machines. This enterprise of transforming the living seems Satanic, insofar as it transgresses boundaries and mixes what should have remained separate. The whole aesthetic of science fiction films crosses the medieval bestiary with the most advanced technology: gargoyles and griffons stuffed with electronics, animalized mutants endowed with fangs and claws, metallic structures covered with hair, winged robots, and so on. (In a famous novel by Clifford D. Simak, the dogs that have seized power give Jenkins, a seven-thousand-year-old robot who serves as their major domo, a birthday present: a new, scintillating suit of armour; but he is so intimidated that at first he does not dare to put it on.[13]) If some disciplines fascinate or frighten us – cloning, nanotechnologies – that is because they feed or confirm our craziest dreams – immortality, omnipotence, or ubiquity – and sketch out a post-human world endowed with an unprecedented metaphysical status. By freeing us from all limits, they allow us to glimpse an exit from the human condition, a scenario that is as seductive as it is naïve. In this case, the danger arises from a puerile desire to triumph over all obstacles. The demonization of technology is only a reversal of the progressivist dream turned into a nightmare.

Thus it is desirable that researchers initiate younger generations into the beauties of scientific work so that they can deepen their understanding of the great word 'knowledge', which Claudel defined as a way of being born together into truth. 'What would it be like to chase a beam of light?' Einstein asked. Science is also poetry, an intuitive grasp of objects, an art of constructing bridges between domains that no one had previously connected; it is fiction, spirituality. How can we reconcile it with opinion? How can we help rediscover the emancipatory goals that were from the outset its reasons for being? By cutting the umbilical cord that binds it to the great consortia or laboratories and makes people suspect it of collusion (but then the problem of public financing for research arises). By putting everything, even the most arduous scientific knowledge, at the level of everyone, by promoting intelligent interchange among scientists and the lay public, by restoring to public opinion a taste for innovation. And especially by destroying the myth of science's omnipotence, which has, in the course of three centuries, made it the substitute for faith and which continues to nourish the trends that appear the most hostile to its propagation.

Scientists tell us that . . .

An astonishing observation: whereas we require ruthless self-examination of many scientists, we still do so in terms of science. It is under its aegis that a new obscurantism is developing, borne by the idolatry of mathematics. For instance, an Internet site devoted to 'ethical cuisine' and to the misdeeds of eating meat explains that 'the production of a kilo of veal emits as much greenhouse gas as a car trip of 220 kilometres'.[14] By what procedure was a result of such precision arrived at, and is it possible to provide a detailed description of this operation that begins with a slice of veal and ends with a car trip? (Always this obsession with the car, as if the true enemy of the ecology movement were human mobility. Let us recall that in France, the Vichy government was the great promoter of the bicycle for everyone, summer and winter, the car being reserved for doctors, members of the militia, and the police. Sequestration for the people, nomadism for the elites. On the scale of a city like Paris, it is clear that the whole policy of the Green Party's elected officials consists in paralysing traffic, at the price of increasing the pollution produced by thousands of vehicles caught in traffic jams. And that is just for starters: we are promised that the lanes along the banks of the Seine and on the ring road will be closed in the near future, and henceforth opened to bicycles and roller skates.) This is a shell game: the confusion of progress with positivism is denounced, but the better to retain the latter's unbridled penchant for quantification! Reason is battled by aping rationality: recourse to computerized models, the invocation of the scientist as an authority figure, the belief in the grandeur of statistics as if numbers were the mathematical translation of truth. The goal of all this gibberish based on fractions and percentages is to make irrefutable propositions. Whereas the scientific act *par excellence* is to say 'I don't know', the new pedants claim to have always known everything and to be beyond any possible challenge.

One example among many: a philosopher once again seeking to combat the damage done by the packaging of yogurt writes: 'It has been calculated that a 125 gram package of strawberry yogurt sold in Stuttgart in 1995 has travelled 9,115 kilometres, if we add the transportation of the milk, that of the strawberries grown in Poland, that of the aluminium in the label, the distance involved in distributing it, etc.'[15] Or again, to continue the food metaphor: 'The average forkful of dinner travels 1,500 miles to reach your lips.'[16] A strange claim: one imagines a group of foodstuffs crossing continents before arriving – cold, of course – in eaters' mouths. What is the purpose of this insane calculation? To paralyse possible objectors! Columns of numbers are lined up the way other people line up tanks to prove their arguments. At the same time that scientism is condemned, it is asked to guarantee us an unconquerable position. The mad collusion of calculation and ideology and the great sophistication of certain discourses seek to reduce opponents to silence and serve as models that can be reproduced indefinitely.

'Scientists tell us that . . .': that is how most of the ecologists' admonishments begin. The militant expert: that is the new type of activist shaped by associations all of whose erudition is put exclusively in the service of politics. Taking over from the extreme left-wing expert on economics, this new type claims to be a living encyclopaedia of the Earth's woes, has at his disposal an avalanche of data on every problem, and constantly peppers us with his theorems. He knows infinitely more than the best of you and can always come up with a bit of information, some detail, that will shut you up. His chief qualification is a diploma in intimidation. Let us recall that, according to Karl Popper, pseudo-sciences are to be reproached, not for being mistaken, but for always being right, for being impermeable to denials.[17] And let us remember that every discipline has its simplified double in a form accessible to all: numerology for mathematics, astrology for astronomy, alchemy for chemistry, and creationism for the theory of evolution, not to mention all the countless variants of alternative medicines. To base a demonstration on a battery of unverifiable or imaginary additions is to substitute indoctrination for respect for the facts and to harm the cause of the environment; the result thus obtained will always be open to challenge by another, cleverer mathematician. Science is reproached less for its methods than for the naïve optimism that has been grafted onto it, that of an absolute mastery over life, of an illusory divinity restored to humans. People forget that in the work of Jules Verne, Auguste Comte, and Victor Hugo, science was not merely domination and exploitation but above all astonishment and admiration. To counterfeit its methods by plastering a totalizing ideology over it is to mock its spirit. Burying public opinion under myriads of numbers does not enlighten the understanding. One shudders to imagine the decisions that might be made, on the basis of purely partisan hypotheses, by an ecological International Penal Tribunal like the one proposed by the Bolivian president, Evo Morales, and supported in France by the leftist politician Jean-Luc Mélenchon.

The fourth copernican revolution

In a famous parallel, Sigmund Freud compared his work to a new Copernican revolution: the first one showed the Earth to be 'a tiny fragment of a cosmic system of scarcely imaginable vastness' and not the centre of the universe; the second, with Darwin, described humans as descending from apes and not as engendered by God. The third, psychoanalysis, expropriated the self from conscious life and proved to it that it is not master in its own house but is instead tossed back and forth by unconscious drives and the pressures of the superego.[18] A fourth blow to our pride has been recently inflicted: we are no longer the rulers of the world but living beings among others who have usurped their place and must abdicate 'their imaginary royalty' (Montaigne). Human beings have been ousted from their privileged position, the world was not created for them: swine, Porphyry already said in the third century, were not made to be eaten by us any more than we were conceived to serve as food for crocodiles. Sobriety, modesty, and moderation: that is the new ethics to be opposed to technological hubris. We are asked to control our addiction to oil, to restrain our appetites, to put an end to waste. *But moderation is still praised immoderately.* Simplicity and restraint cannot be the last words of the human adventure, especially when this programme of exhaustion is pursued with such disturbing enthusiasm.

The borderline between the natural and the artificial never ceases to move, but it never disappears, and each generation modifies it to suit itself without ever doing away with it. Human beings, those 'denatured animals' (Vercors), are never at ease in their environment: they are always too prominent or too withdrawn, exceeding their prerogatives and constantly reorganizing knowledge and power. Development, yes, but not at the price of compromising the future, of destroying landscapes and cultures, or permanently damaging whole regions: in Canada, for example, native peoples have won the right to veto projects to build dams, drill for gas or oil, or install oil pipelines. Europe has established protected natural areas in which human activities become compatible with protecting the environment. In any event, when an industrial, mining, or hydroelectric project is planned, it is better to involve the neighbouring populations and local organizations in it rather than conspiring behind their backs. The oil spill off Louisiana in the summer of 2010 is an illustration of this *a contrario*: although they had been hard hit by the explosion of the Deepwater Horizon platform and the long-lasting pollution of the coastline, shrimp and lobster fishermen did not demand that offshore drilling by BP be halted, but rather that security measures be strengthened and a decent indemnity be paid. For them, the coexistence of fishing and oil production is a good thing whose advantages they want without the disadvantages. Does the government in Ottawa want to launch a development project in the Canadian far north? Most of the Native American tribes are in favour of it, provided that certain strict conditions are met. The ecologists, of course, are against it.

In general, three ways of dealing with nature are distinguished: preservation, conservation, and reconstitution.[19] The great American and Canadian national parks, imagined in the United States by John Muir, correspond to the first principle, and reserve vast areas of wildlife: the most beautiful thing in America, apart from its emblematic cities, is its wide open spaces, its immense deserts, its forests with gigantic trees. Conservation consists in developing a territory's resources without doing any irreversible damage to it, by means of a policy of intelligent care. Finally, one can work to restore something that has been destroyed or diminished: peat fields in the Ardennes, eroded soils in Manitoba, marshes in Iraq, coral reefs in Antigua, the taiga in Russia. In France, forested areas have doubled in size since 1827, and now cover 28.6 per cent of the territory, or 15.7 million hectares. In comparison, in 1690, there remained in England and Wales only 1,200,000 hectares of forests after two centuries of intensive tree felling. Many ecosystems can recuperate in twenty years, and damage can be reversed: for instance, the hole in the ozone layer over Antarctica has shrunk by 30 per cent as compared to its size in 2006,[20] though we do not know exactly why. As for human intrusion, it can be beneficial. The parts of the Amazon forest transformed by human presence have a richer variety of flora and fauna than the virgin parts.[21]

At the walker's empirical level, it is astonishing to note how quickly flora and fauna can re-establish themselves in large cities as soon as humans leave them room to do so. Consider the fact that the fox is returning to the suburbs of Paris, that birds of prey have taken up residence in Notre Dame's towers, and that seagulls nest on the capital's roofs, abandoning the seaside to feed on the waste generated by the Rungis market. Some great hotels in Paris engage falconers who train buzzards, eagles, and hawks to drive away pigeons. In Berlin, raccoons are proliferating around the Bundestag, moles live under the lawns of the Reichstag, gulls fish in the waters of the Spree, and eagles are once again hunting in the city's parks. London has been invaded by the ring-necked parakeet, which can tolerate very cold weather, devours the contents of bird-feeders, attacks weaker species, and deafens residents with its squawking. Thousands of monkeys live on the roofs of Dacca, the capital of Bangladesh, forcing residents to protect their homes with iron grates: the monkeys, which are very aggressive, steal clothes hung out to dry and give them back only in exchange for food – failing which they tear them up. A noble tomcat ambling across a street in the Marais quarter of Paris on a fine spring day – staying on the pedestrian crossing, taking his time, sure of his rights – is a delightful sight.

Saving the spirit of exploration

All this assumes a new relationship of friendship and collaboration with the world, but not a renunciation.

Clearly, we have to fight for the creation of natural reserves that cannot be touched and for making the oceans the common property of humanity. But human activity cannot be reduced to that of a gardener. Affectionate concern for parks and beaches, and the imperative protection of species threatened by extinction, is compatible with the development of other parts of the globe. In France, up to the 1970s, hunting consisted in shooting anything that moved, in eliminating every kind of game, one after another. Introducing the requirement of a permit turned hunting into a matter of knowing and respecting the world of wildlife, and helped repopulate whole regions with wild boars, deer, chamois, and birds. The problematic reappearance in the Alps of wolves coming from Italy, and the relocation of bears from Slovenia into the Pyrenees, are part of the same process. If bull-fighting were to be abolished in Spain, the breed of bulls that are used in the arenas would disappear as well; if we stopped eating meat, the reasons for raising calves, steers, hogs, and chickens would vanish, and so would these animals. That is an outcome accepted by some animal rights militants, for whom the extinction of categories of animals held in slavery – ducks raised for their livers, cattle, sheep, and fowl – is preferable to their being exploited by humans.[22] Better not to be born than to live miserably. Apart from the fact that the animals involved are never asked their opinion on this matter – that is the inherent paternalism of this movement – it is after all strange that the solution advocated for eliminating the suffering of living beings is their disappearance, pure and simple, just as certain radical ecologists desire the disappearance of the human race. If we must no longer use animals or domesticate them for labour or our entertainment, that is, close zoos, circuses, aviaries, research laboratories, riding schools, and so on, then all we can do is protect living animals by ensuring that they will not reproduce and will be the last of their kind (that is the position taken by people like Tom Regan and Gary Francione). Thus we arrive at this paradox: instead of exploring new forms of coexistence, the defenders of animal rights advocate animals' slow, painless extermination.

There are several ways of using nature, and our mistake is to have neglected some of them in favour of a relationship of utility or exploitation. We are simultaneously outside nature and inside it, embedded in it and looking down on it from above. The world is not our due; it is conferred on us as an obligation so that we can transmit it to following generations, if possible in a better condition. 'We do not inherit the earth from our parents, we borrow it from our children,' as an Indian proverb has it. But engaging in a dialogue with nature does not prevent us from taming or cultivating it. Celebrating the shimmering beauty of the world, the fluffiness of clouds, the splendour of the oceans and the aurora borealis, or admiring the incredible profusion of minuscule life-forms, does not imply a renunciation of all industrial or agricultural activity. We will continue to battle diseases (which are very 'natural'), the mutations of viruses or bacteria, torrential rains, extreme cold, and hurricanes; we will also continue to build cities, probably ones demanding less energy, and intelligent homes; we will not stop constructing dams, drilling wells, or digging mines, even if we do so more discerningly. Experimentation is not incompatible with contemplation: they are two different orders that we can re-equilibrate without conflating them. While waiting for our species to colonize space, to spread to other galaxies and make them habitable for humans,[23] and also for the fusion of human and machine, we have pleaded for a new kind of progress that is self-critical and aware of its ambivalence. Civilization creates as many problems as it resolves, and the solutions it provides generate further miseries in turn. There is no single, federating progress, but rather localized forms of progress that are themselves paradoxical and that also produce regressions. That was already known to Jules Verne, for instance; for him, an advance is always followed by a decline in a kind of eternal return: the same eruption that creates an atoll amid the seas later destroys it, and the romance of science is as overwhelming as it is exhilarating.[24] We are sobered believers, perhaps, but being sobered does not mean being disillusioned, and it has never led anyone to reject electricity or to return to horse-drawn wagons (except for a few spoiled children of the affluent society). Why should we deprive ourselves of the countless outcomes of a discovery? Anyone who has undergone a successful surgical operation, has been saved by an antibiotic, or got rid of a headache by taking aspirin, knows what the word 'advance' means. Renouncing inconsiderate destruction does not entail renouncing research. The choice is not between an intact Nature that slowly recovers from human intrusions and a devastating productivism that forges, pierces, and disfigures, but between a process of regression and development lucidly embraced with all its risks and benefits.

Georges Canguilhem drew a distinction between light, as the engine of history in the eighteenth century, and heat, as the symbol of the nineteenth century. Heat depends on fossil fuels, that is, on non-renewable resources. In this respect, our age, at least in the West, lacks both heat and light; it is low-consumption, like the light bulbs of the same name, in a universe of entropy. Ecologism is a philosophy of twilight, of the pale and wan. Will genetic engineering soon allow us to develop a mosquito that can sterilize the anopheles mosquitoes that spread malaria? That would be a prodigious invention capable of eradicating one of the worst scourges of our time. Immediately the censors throw fits, associations mobilize: no genetically modified organisms! Does the Intergovernmental Panel on Climate Change (IPCC) propose developing techniques for guiding the climate by means of geo-engineering and partially blocking solar radiation? The planet's puritans are indignant: imagining that this might work, imagining for a moment that things might improve, that one of these techniques, however far-fetched, might have a positive effect? For our inquisitors, that would be totally unacceptable: everything always has to go from bad to worse, and we have to suffer . . . Another pious wish: suppose that a bio-technology laboratory discovered a miraculous synthetic product or an alternative hydro-carbon that could substitute for petroleum and nuclear power; then imagine that genetic engineering could create a human being with a smaller ecological foot-print, one that was better adapted to the planet's limited resources. Immediately the Green lobbies would rise up, seeing androids attacking humanity or intelligent matter crushing its creator. How does one recognize an ecologist? By the fact that he is against everything: carbon, even with CO_2 capture, natural gas, shale gas, ethanol, diesel, nuclear power, petrol, dams, trucks, high-speed trains, cars, planes . . . Once again the true desire of this movement is not to safeguard nature but to punish human beings.

The Lisbon Earthquake

On 1 November 1755, an earthquake, followed by a tidal wave and a fire that lasted five days, devastated the city of Lisbon, leaving between 50,000 and 100,000 dead. The event was not merely physical but metaphysical: it challenged the optimism of the Enlightenment and elicited three kinds of responses. The first was that of Voltaire: at the age of sixty, the most famous outlaw in Europe found his convictions battered by the quake and expressed his anger and revolt in a famous 'Poem on the Disaster in Lisbon':

Deceived philosophers, who cry: All is well,
Hurry to contemplate these dreadful ruins,
These debris, these tatters, these wretched ashes,
These women and children piled on one another,
Under these broken marbles, these scattered
    limbs,
A hundred thousand unfortunates whom the
    earth devours,
Who, bleeding, lacerated, and still trembling,
Buried under their roofs are ending without
    succour,
In the horror of torments, their lamentable lives
    [. . .]
Will you say, seeing this heap of victims:
God is avenged, their death is the price of their
    crime!
What sin, what crime have these children
    committed,
Broken and bleeding on their mothers' breast
    [. . .]
Someday all will be well, that is our hope.
Everything is well today, that is the illusion.[25]

For Voltaire, evil exists, and in two forms: in
Nature and in humans. The euphoria of the beginning of the eighteenth century has to be attenuated.
If there is a God, He is either terribly cruel or
totally powerless. The hope of a reconciliation of
humanity with itself under the aegis of commerce,
education, and tolerance is abandoned or at least
relativized. To Voltaire's pessimism, Rousseau
retorts, with a strange form of good sense:

Acknowledge that if nature had not gathered there
twenty thousand buildings of six or seven storeys,
and if the residents of this great city had been
more equally distributed and lived in smaller
buildings, the damage would have been much
smaller and perhaps non-existent. Everyone would
have fled at the first tremor, and the following day

they would have been seen twenty leagues away
from there, as happy as if nothing had happened.
But they had to stay, stubbornly clinging to their
tumbledown dwellings and exposing themselves
to further tremors because what one leaves behind
is worth more than what one can take along. How
many unfortunate wretches died in this disaster
because one wanted to take his clothes, another
his papers, and another his money?[26]

Here Rousseau targets all the flaws he detests in
civilization: people's avarice, their property instinct,
and especially the absurd need to gather together
in cities, with all the corruption that entails. Contrary to what one might expect, he thinks not like
a fatalist, but like a modern. With a little reason
and foresight, the horror could have been avoided.
The world is not absurd, as Candide imagines, it
is just poorly organized.

Two famous figures pick up where Rousseau left
off: Immanuel Kant wrote a short monograph in
which he attributes earthquakes to gases concentrated in gigantic caverns under the earth, an initial
attempt to explain them by reference to natural
and not supernatural phenomena. But the most
sensible reaction was that of the Marquis of
Pombal, the Portuguese king's prime minister: he
had Lisbon reconstructed in accord with an urban
plan designed to minimize earthquake damage:
large squares, broad avenues, lower buildings. He
tested model houses by subjecting them day and
night to the passage of heavily loaded wagons that
produced shaking like that of an earthquake. Thus
was seismology born.[27] Outraged stupefaction,
prudent humility, and rational resistance to chaos:
these are the three responses that can be made to
catastrophes. Faced with disaster, we can abandon
ourselves to invective or show ourselves to be

stronger than what seeks to destroy us. Chaos is also creative; it makes us intelligent and generates unprecedented configurations, in accord with the theory proposed in 1830 by the famous palaeontologist and anatomist Georges Cuvier.[28] The cosmic fury of the stars and insane eruptions of matter give birth to new forms of life.

Sade, that great buccaneer opposing the optimism of the Enlightenment, demonstrated the point in a provocative way: the sole commandment made by Nature is crime in all its forms. Nature is an evil stepmother who squanders gigantic forces and engulfs her own creations in her gyrations. According to Sade, killing is a matter not of eliminating an irreplaceable life but of lending oneself to this law of metamorphoses that swallows up forms to make them re-emerge differently. Human beings are just accidents, loquacious parasites whose extinction should have no more effect on the course of the universe than the death of a fly. Was Sade a precursor of our modern activists on behalf of the Earth? He probably would have found them very tame, but he would have applauded present-day eco-fascism and its projects for eliminating the human race. Gaia is neither good nor bad: she teaches us no lessons. Human beings are alone!

Part III

The Great Ascetic Regression

Part III

The Great Atomic Regression

7

Humanity on a Strict Diet

Frugality is like honesty, it's a poor, wretched virtue suitable only for small societies of good, peaceful people who are quite willing to be poor so long as they are not bothered; but in great, active nations [. . .] frugality is an indolent, dreamy virtue that does not employ workers and is consequently very useless in a country devoted to business [. . .]. What idiot, if he had a good bed, would have slept outside?
    Voltaire, *Dictionnaire philosophique*, art. 'Luxury'

On 30 August 1755, Voltaire sent a letter to Rousseau to thank him for his work entitled *A Discourse on the Origin and Basis of Inequality Among Men*:

I am in receipt, Monsieur, of your new book against the human race. I thank you for it; you will please the people you set right and you will not correct them. It is impossible to paint in brighter colours the horrors of human society from which ignorance and weakness hope to draw so many consolations. No one has ever employed so much wit in trying to make us into animals. On reading your work, one feels like going on all fours.

Voltaire's remarks are as incisive as they are unfair. The author of *Émile* notes a gap between the progress of the sciences and the arts and that of the human species. Perfectibility in the destiny of the individual does not go hand in hand with the advance of civilization. To reconcile the human heart and human reason in society, we should take as our model, if we can, the rectitude of Nature. Rousseau wants virtuous and austere citizens who are capable of defending their homeland, while Voltaire wants people who are happy, polite, and brilliant. Rousseau attacks the luxury that deprives the poor and leads to the corruption of taste and morals. Beyond the wounded gravity of the one and the haughty brio of the other, their quarrel still resonates today among the partisans of a lavish life and those who militate for rigour, the prophets of rusticity and frugality.

An ethics of renunciation

'To change the world, change life.' To this formula inherited from Rimbaud and the communist tradition, ecologism adds a fundamental corrective: we have to change our lives in order to preserve the world, to save it from the scourge known as productivism. For ecologism, the domestic becomes immediately political, and we can permanently inflect the course of societies by turning off lights, turning down the heating, and becoming economical and if possible vegetarian, which would reduce emissions of greenhouse gases. Since our mode of production is destroying the planet's resources, the first thing we have to limit is our desires, and a sense of restriction must be inculcated in everyone. The household and home are not neutral or insignificant places where we enjoy ourselves with those close to us; they are the epicentre of crime *par excellence*. It is there, in the warmth of the family, that the conspiracy against the Earth is fomented, in a mixture of negligence, greed, and dependency that constitutes the heart of civilized corruption. High school students, retirees, fishermen, farmers, engineers, employees – we are all potential killers who subsist only by destroying.

> A society that is incapable of allowing the majority of its members to earn a living by honest work and that condemns them to act against their conscience by making them accomplices in the banality of evil in order to survive is in a profound crisis. That is, however, precisely the case in our late modernity, from fishermen who can get along only by massacring life in the depths of the sea to farmers who are destroying the soil that feeds us, plus energetic managers who have become killers.[1]

This amounts, as we have seen, to a massive restoration of Original Sin under the auspices of the extinction of species, the collapse of marine ecosystems, and rising temperatures. The slightest act – eating a cutlet, turning on a radiator, letting the water run while you brush your teeth (at school, children are taught that this is a bad thing for the planet) – is heavy with unexpected consequences. A society based on growth, its detractors claim, is criminal for three reasons: 'It engenders a rise in inequalities and injustices, it creates a largely illusory well-being, and even for the privileged it creates, not a convivial society, but an anti-society sick of its wealth.'[2] We live worse than ever because water, air, and the environment are deteriorating:

> For some years now, our Western societies have found themselves in the situation of an individual who, in order to earn 3,000 euros, has to adopt a mode of life that is so unnatural that he has to spend 2,000 euros in a desperate effort to compensate for its catastrophic effects on his physical and mental health.[3]

The past century has in fact invented a phenomenon that drives all camps crazy and condenses in its temples all the ignominy of the human race: consumer society. Henry Miller, describing the United States in the 1950s, called it the 'air-conditioned nightmare', while in the 1930s Georges Duhamel, cursing the invention of the cinema in America, spoke of an 'entertainment for helots'. Today, countless writers on both the right and the left rail against those 'who live and think like swine'.[4]

The consumer combines three radical defects: he behaves like a predator by contributing to the looting of the planet's resources. He is an anthropological monstrosity, a Pavlovian being driven by rudimentary instincts of hunger and satisfaction. Worse yet, he is a kind of Sisyphus doomed to eternal dissatisfaction, repeating the process over and over. Prey to artificial needs that make him the slave of his own well-being – that is Tocqueville's critique, which had already been voiced by Benjamin Constant – he sees only his material interest, to the detriment of his freedom and of the common concern. In short, every discourse agrees in denouncing him: vulgar, selfish, wasteful, he insults our ideas of justice, equality, and beauty. '[M]ass society', Theodor Adorno said, 'did not first produce the trash for the customers, but the customers themselves.'[5] In other words, the buyer in turn is transformed into human junk: that is the terrible impact of commodification on subjectivity. It engenders robots that all desire the same objects before moving on to others of which they will soon grow tired as well. Rousseau had already grasped this perverse mechanism of insatiability:

> [A]mong men in society, other things are involved: it is primarily a matter of providing for necessities and then for the superfluous; afterward come delights and then immense wealth and then subjects and then slaves; there is not a moment of respite: what is most singular is that the less natural and urgent the needs, the more the

passions increase, and worse yet, so does the power of satisfying them.[6]

Progress is a curse: it forbids us to be content with our condition, makes us avid for the slightest innovation, and the phenomenon is amplified in a mass society in which millions of individuals are in the grip of the demon of rapacity. 'The superfluous is something very necessary,' said Voltaire. But this appetite is both diabolical and mediocre; apart from the fact that it gives rise to a factitious abundance, it arouses the desire of the masses, who aspire in vain to equal the affluence of the most prosperous groups. Fortunately, in the depths of the abyss, redemption is possible: we can mend our arrogant ways by adopting an extremely ascetic code of behaviour. 'Decrease is our destiny. We will not escape it! We have lived like princes, the party's over.'[7]

Here we have to examine a rhetorical figure that is frequently employed in this kind of literature, and that was first extensively used by Christianity: less is more. The last on Earth will be the first in Heaven, the fools of this world will be the wise in the next, blessed are the simple-minded for they will be golden. This way of thinking in antonyms, the notion that evil is a hidden good that will be revealed at some later point, constitutes above all a machine for legitimating a state of affairs. Apparent iniquity masks a promise whose fulfilment we have to be able to wait for. This kind of reasoning was to be very fertile in the works of the Church Fathers and of Leibniz, but also in those of the theorists of the 'invisible hand', from Mandeville to Hayek, without forgetting totalitarian regimes that made it a fearsome weapon for subjecting people. In environmentalist propaganda, this kind of logic consists in reversing values: in transforming consumerism into a dreadful pathology, 'the greatest weapon of mass destruction'[8] invented by the human mind, in order to make acceptable neo-pauperism, that is, 'detachment with regard to the spirit of profit' (*Manifeste pour une décroissance conviviale*, 2009). Since wealth leads to despair, need ought to elicit a return of hope. In fact, the progress of the material standard of living in the United States has been accompanied by an undeniable decrease in real happiness among most Americans.[9] Conclusion: since having more means being less, having less will mean being more! A marvellous acrobatic act: we have to voluntarily deprive ourselves in order to enrich ourselves spiritually. Subtraction as amplification!

Impoverish yourself!

For those who are alarmed to see many regions of Africa, for example, still suffering from poverty and anarchy, our apostles of destitution offer a major corrective: Africans are in reality ahead of us, because they have a long tradition of deprivation from which we should draw the inspiration for ridding ourselves of our bad habits: 'Africa, help our mental development. Africa, help Europe enter a new history [. . .]. Africa can teach the West how to adapt to frugality.'[10] Let us ignore the paternalism of this apostrophe: it sounds too much like the wealthy explaining to the needy that having money doesn't make people happy. Happy are the deprived who don't have servants to supervise (or to screw), homes to maintain, taxes to pay, fortunes to manage. Professors of poverty, that is what sub-Saharan peoples are reduced to. Senegalese, Malians, Nigerians, and Congolese who are eager to emerge from underdevelopment will know what to think of this view worthy of an obsolete neo-colonialism. It really is a matter of readapting our mental apparatus on the model of destitute societies that are capable of greater resilience when confronted with torments and restrictions. 'Americans and Europeans have to reduce their consumption. To be blunt, they have to impoverish themselves. They are beginning to do so, *nolens volens*, because of the economic crisis, which arose from their forgetting the environment through an over-consumption that has maintained an excessive indebtedness.'[11]

A slogan is all the rage among Green neo-Puritans: voluntary simplicity. Inherited from the American writer Henry David Thoreau, an adept of 'downshifting' and abandoning cities, encouraged by Tolstoy and Gandhi, adopted in France by figures such as Lanza del Vasto, a militant for non-violence, it is founded on this aphorism: 'We have to live more simply so that others may simply live' (Gandhi). On the pretext that rich societies have to moderate their desires, we are hearing more and more ascetic voices telling us that we should love indigence, cherish it as our most precious possession. It alone is 'convivial' and teaches us how to get along with less, in togetherness and joy. True wealth consists in restoring the dignity of privation. 'The organization of the economy with a view to well-being is the major obstacle to well-being,' Ivan Illich was already saying in 1973.[12] Here the use of oxymoron triumphs: are we going, then, to celebrate 'happy frugality', 'just austerity', 'joyous sobriety', 'frugal abundance', and – why not? – 'delightful poverty', 'amusing death', and 'pleasant famine'? It's as if those lauding the new precariousness were competing to see who can juxtapose the most incompatible terms. What is an oxymoron? A miracle worker, no more nor less, that makes it possible to escape an embarrassing situation. In place of the eradication of poverty, the programme pursued by all political camps, ecologism proposes the voluntary reduction of everyone to a Third World standard of living. Since material wealth is synonymous with moral poverty, material poverty can only encourage spiritual opulence. A marvellous syllogism: the diminution of goods should result in an amplification of social ties. A deficit in possessions should be followed by a growth in being. 'The reduction sought is also an increase in health, well-being, and *joie de vivre*.'[13] To live better, we have to separate ourselves from our possessions. 'The few families who live without television are not to be pitied.'[14] Maybe! But it is a choice freely made, not an obligation imposed by scarcity. Specifically, to carry out this great project of social disinfection, you will need to get rid of your car, take showers instead of baths (and the showers must be limited to four minutes; little hour-glasses are sold for the purpose), stop buying imported fruit and vegetables, practise 'locavorism' (that is, eat only locally produced products), decrease or even halt your consumption of meat and fish, avoid the elevator and even the refrigerator: 'The refrigerator would be replaced by a cold room, a trip to the Antilles by cycling in the Cévennes, the vacuum cleaner by the broom, and meat-eating by vegetarianism.'[15]

Each of us has to kill the frenetic consumer within us, for he is the scruffy wretch who through his greed is causing the melting of the polar icecaps, the rise in sea level, tremors in the Earth's crust, acid rain, and who knows what else. Thus we have to rid ourselves of a vice that is eating away at us: abundance. The choice to live differently – that is, without television, car, computer, or microwave – is difficult but exhilarating:

> It is the choice to live today rather than to sacrifice present life to consumption or the accumulation of values without value, to the construction of a career plan that is supposed to make tomorrow satisfying, or scrimping to complete a retirement savings plan intended to calm the fear of not having enough.[16]

How these unpleasant matters are wrapped up in sweet words! We sacrifice in the expectation of receiving a benefit, and as if by magic, what we give up will be restored to us hundredfold. What is the difference between yesterday's preachers and today's? The latter talk like the affable organizers of the Club

Méditerranée, using the epithet 'cool' to sugar-coat their slightest remarks. Are you cold in the winter? Put on a sweater, for heaven's sake, instead of turning up the radiator, and go to bed early, Yves Cochet, a deputy in the French National Assembly, tells us: 'We have to manage to live with 50 per cent less electricity [. . .]. We have to take maximum advantage of daylight, put on a sweater rather than turning up the heat by three degrees!' And our friend of humanity further suggests a surtax on those who make excessive use of electricity and heating systems. Are we going to set up police brigades that are charged with switching off electricity and will establish a curfew for the French and Germans? What great people! In 2011 the ecology-orientated mayor of Paris's second arrondissement decreed a day of vegetarian meals in school cafeterias. An excellent step. But why decree it instead of proposing it? What is worrisome about ecologism is that it energetically insinuates itself into the most intimate aspects of our lives, our eating habits and our clothing, the better to control them. On reading its recommendations, we can almost hear the heavy door of a dungeon closing behind us. In any case, 'the capitalist model is going to self-destruct', 'the era of consumption and comfort is coming to an end' (Harald Welzer), thanks to the various scourges that are striking us, and that's all to the better: 'We still adhere to our cardinal criterion of waste and irresponsibility by driving our cars to work every morning, wasting our time in fitness centres on weekends, or jamming into aeroplanes to go rot our brains someplace on the other side of the Earth.'[17] But especially: 'Most of our contemporaries are themselves broken. How could they create healthy, normal children?'[18]

Let us linger a moment over these lines, which betray a rare hatred of the human race! How can we propose a revolution in our way of life if we begin by rejecting and despising our fellow humans? In the name of what principle can we judge humanity as a whole without including ourselves in this pejorative judgement? The project here is authoritarian: we have to impose material difficulty, indeed, return to candles and horse-drawn vehicles, and present this as an unprecedented advance for the human race. As Sylvia Pérez-Vitoria writes:

> Returning to candles refers to a technological return to the past [. . .]. Let us note first of all that most of the world's peasants still use candles (or at least oil lamps). [. . .] If we returned to candles, the great majority of humanity would continue to live as it does now, with far less pressure on its resources and its crops. [. . .] Even if the return to candles were not complete – we've already seen that in history – all in all that wouldn't be so bad![19]

Our knights battling for a reversal of growth will have to deploy all the oratorical talent of nineteenth-century bosses explaining to their workers that higher salaries and more time off would promote immorality and drunkenness, and that they were going to have to be content with their stinking hovels, their miserable salaries, and their terrifyingly long work days. By setting the norms of life by reference to the most deprived, our virtuous inquisitors are proposing an unprecedented concept: cheerful need. This comes at the right time, given the crisis that Europe is currently experiencing, which leaves educated young people on the margins of the system and prompts angry riots almost everywhere: it is more exciting when one has to scrimp on everything, electricity, meat, clothing, travel, leisure activities, telling oneself that in doing so one is helping save the planet. *This is the art of inserting individual stinginess into cosmic altruism.* In this sense, reversing growth is not the programme of an enlightened minority that wants to halt the mad convoy of progress but the iron law of a financial capitalism that penalizes the lower and middle classes: it's a matter of transforming necessity into a free choice. The Greens are adapting to the new economic situation that allows a minority of privileged people greatly to increase their fortunes while others are supposed to tighten their belts. They confirm the blocked situation of younger generations that can no longer be sure that they will live better than their parents did, and have to resign themselves to this misfortune.

Long before Rousseau, the theme of frugal abundance was popularized in a period of great poverty by the French poet Jean de Meun in his *Roman de la Rose* (thirteenth century). He imagined a state of nature in the distant past, where tastes were simple and the Earth provided in profusion everything that people needed. Humans lived in great happiness before the appearance of an army of vices – deception, pride, covetousness, envy, etc. – sowed discord and gave rise to agriculture, a taste for gold, private property, and power. Thus there was a land of plenty until the Fall drove out all the inhabitants.[20] Today, 'happy sobriety' (Pierre Rabhi),[21] frugal life 'with limited desires', has to be chosen serenely. Parsimony and ethically equitable candle-stubs. Juxtaposing the word 'convivial' with 'austerity' produces a semantic balm that fools no one, as we saw in the former 'popular democracies' of the Soviet bloc, which were neither popular nor democratic. There is something nauseating about these statements that recall the worst newspaper adverts or the Stalinist slogans mocked by George Orwell. Here we are in the register of fallacious consolations. If people want to make us swallow the bitter potion of rigour, they might at least tell us so frankly.

The preachers of austerity

Thus need has to be made palatable, the way we put a red nose on a clown. The magazine *La décroissance* calls itself 'The Journal of *Joie de Vivre*', no doubt ironically. The bigots want mad laughter and gaiety to mask the ascetic plague they are propagating! A mystery of transubstantiation! You lack everything, you live meagrely, but you will enjoy a whiff of beatitude and you will help fight global warming. There is an ascetic intoxication, a sensual pleasure in depriving oneself and getting along with the strict minimum. Have more lively stylites, more jovial flagellants, ever been seen? It is true that the ambition is no longer to improve one's soul, to expand one's body and mind, as the Ancients urged, but to survive the disaster constituted by the Industrial Revolution. And survival adapts to cramped desires, shrivelled ambitions, stunted pleasures. Humans are insane in the excess of their appetites, and their madness consists in desiring what they do not have. 'I'm sorry, but humanity is mad. It can't go on much longer: at 9 billion, we die! This planet is going to become more and more violent for us. Either we take that into account, or we crash and have Fukushima on a large scale.'[22]

According to our Robespierres of the candle, we have to give up luxury, consumerism, and exotic travel to make a tiny but decisive contribution to the proper functioning of the universe. In order to rid us of our bad habits, a 'Transition movement'[23] offers us decontamination spaces analogous to withdrawal programmes for alcoholics and drug addicts: in them, we learn to get used to not depending on petrol, to evolving toward a more economical and self-sufficient way of life. These professors of need are the equivalent of the therapists who treat lottery winners by teaching them to manage their winnings without sinking into mere squandering. But what we give up in the way of superficial desires maintained by advertising and marketing we get back hundredfold in joy and authentic relationships. Just listen to the pack of killjoys preaching in a thousand ways the urgency of impoverishing ourselves. They castigate the insouciance of our fellow citizens who leave on vacations, spreading their carbon imprints to the ends of the Earth, surf on their computers, frenetically tap on their mobile phones, and still drive 4×4s instead of covering their heads in ashes in order to devote themselves to repentance and saving. What do they want? To draw a black mourning veil over all human joys? Do you like to spend your summers far from home? You have to break that bad habit, because tourism mocks the dignity of peoples, destroys cultural diversity, and proves to be harmful to the environment! Do you still like to go skiing in the Alps or the Pyrenees? Our sectarians choke with indignation: do you realize what that luxurious form of recreation costs nature? Snow machines alone emit eight tonnes of CO_2 per hectare.[24] No more skiing, surfing, snowboarding, tobogganing; put away your skis and poles, and forget all-terrain vehicles and motorsports at the coast. You have to stop doing all that. Biking and organic food, nothing else. You used to have fun? Well, now you have to atone for it.

As in monastic orders, poverty is the choice of the essential over the accessory, over the world's mirages. Restriction is described in lyrical terms as a marvellous expansion of the human person. Isn't that what Ivan Illich and André Gorz meant by 'joyous austerity' when they advocated a reduction of needs and the work week in favour of a more diversified social life? In plain English, this is called sugaring the pill. How does a decrease in monetary wealth automatically lead to an improvement of intellectual life? It is one thing to give things up voluntarily, the way monks and saints do, and another to be forced to give them up: 'I am arguing for a renascence of ascetic practices to keep our senses alive in lands devastated by the "show", amid crushing amounts of information, endless advice, intensive diagnostics, therapeutic management, the invention of counsellors, terminal care, and breath-taking speed.'[25] A return to sacrifice, that's what Ivan Illich is demanding, along with a 'techno-fast'. Lots of luck!

But why must everyone live on gruel? Why try to make everyone eat as they did in wartime? We can't help suspecting that this eulogy of impoverished life is dictated less by necessity than by simple hatred for the system, for the 'rampant totalitarianism of globalized consumer society'.[26] Even if it were possible to keep the latter going forever in its present form, it would be preferable to eliminate it, because consumerism's true sin is moral. 'Our way of life is unsustainable ecologically as well as morally. However, even if it could go on indefinitely, it would still be unbearable and it would be desirable to change it.'[27] For such opponents of growth, there is no point in trying to develop this world; they would prefer to eliminate it altogether.

8

The Poverty of Maceration

Greed loses everything by trying to gain everything.
                                        Jean de La Fontaine

So what is this joy that bureaucrats of planetary salvation offer us in place of the Hell of abundance? What might be called the miser's triumph on the cosmic level. Nothing must escape vigilant accounting: we never leave the mean domain of possession for the splendid realm of Being; more than ever we are fascinated by the quantitative. Even our cattle's emissions of intestinal gas contribute to the greenhouse effect. An Australian-American pioneer of the 'kite turbine', Saul Griffith, sadly admits this nasty mania, whereby he went so far as to make ridiculously detailed calculations of the energy consumed by his roll of toilet paper and his electric toothbrush.[1] He can no longer look at an every-day object without seeing the green figures of the energy necessary to make it pass before his eyes.

The sacredness of manure

Consider the case of a Los Angeles cameraman, Dave Chameides, who vowed not to throw away his rubbish during the year 2008 and instead stored it in his cellar, where he showed it to curious visitors. He belongs to the tribe of 'carborexics', those who seek to reduce their carbon imprint at any cost. In his cellar, cartons, paint pots, pizza boxes, plastic bottles, and discarded electronic gear have a second and a third life. On his website, he keeps detailed records of their decomposition: to deal with the problem of odours he has installed a veritable factory for voracious and fecund worms. The latter produce, in addition to compost, a liquid that is good for plants and that he calls 'larva tea'.[2] Worms are becoming very popular in large American and European cities: they are raised for their fertilizing virtues and their beneficial juices. Chameides, a new bard of refuse, describes the metamorphosis of his debris day by day, as if he were hatching a treasure, and boasts that he produces no more than one kilo of rubbish per month instead of two kilos a day, like the average American. A marvellous epic of peelings, a saintliness of rejects. One has to make one's slag a business, become acquainted with the charming little family of annelids. True life is found in the rubbish dump. It's Robinson Crusoe in an apartment; the joy of wading through dirt and muck at home.

'Composting promotes social bonds and creates a new art of living in the city.'[3] Come home with me, I'll show you my maggots! A mystical crisis can be elicited by anything; even a rubbish bin can awaken the soul. In this respect, we have to distinguish between two types of fantasy among ecologists: on the one hand, a scatological fantasy focused on decomposition that begins with sorting rubbish; and, on the other hand, a fantasy focused on lightening, whose aim is to jettison all weight. The first fantasy resembles an inverted form of the hoarding that classical moralists called *avaritia* (from which 'avarice' is derived) and which was one of the seven deadly sins.[4] The utopian theorist Charles Fourier considered a passion for rubbish characteristic of childhood: in his phalanstery, crowds of kids driven by an immoderate taste for dirt are put to work picking up rubbish, emptying septic tanks, and so on. The taste for money has something in common with the passion for refuse and anal retention: it is accumulated when it becomes an end in itself. In the iconography of the Last Judgment, the miser has his purse around his neck even in Hell among the damned. He venerates his moneybag for all eternity.[5] The Green movement would like to transform this insatiable appetite into a virtue, just as economic liberalism counts on the selfishness of individuals to construct a prosperous society. In order to preserve nature, ecologism situates it within a vast computational system in which all telluric forces – winds, sun, hurricanes, tides – are subjected to a strict mathematics. We are no longer in the world of Rousseau or Thoreau, who lauded natural life, but in that of the penny-pincher whose money chest is as large as the whole globe. A vision of the Earth as an impoverished family that has to scrimp on everything in order to get along. A rehabilitation of meanness and stinginess, which, at the beginning of the twenty-first century, have become great civic virtues. Thus proponents of reversing growth are influenced, in spite of themselves, by a utilitarian ethos that obsesses them. Nothing must be thrown away, nothing spent; one's slightest waste must be kept as a treasure. 'Become a tightwad', a PriceMinister ad in the Paris Metro urged. The commercial sprit has contaminated even its most bitter enemies, who speak its language even as they seek to demolish it.

Ecologism seeks to be the revenge of the rural world on an urban civilization that has partially eliminated it. It represents the dream of a community that is close to the earth, that does not have an excessive division of labour, and in which everyone, man or woman, furnishes the share of labour suited to his or her abilities and receives the same benefits. Behind all these pleas can be discerned the touching silhouette of the Amish, with their old-fashioned clothes, their outdated hair-styles, and their horse-drawn buggies. The Amish are in fact the heroes of many activists, who celebrate their rejection of superfluous innovations and sense of local democracy, and offer vacations in this ingenious and hospitable community in Pennsylvania. For instance, a California member of the WWOOF (World Wide Opportunities on Organic Farms), a network of organic farms founded by neo-hippies on the principle of rejecting chemical fertilizers, pesticides, and mechanized agriculture (horses are used to till the fields), asserts that:

> Our vegetables are full of vitality because they respect the Earth's cycle of fertility. Biodynamic preparations allow our vegetables to be receptive to cosmic and mineral influences. [. . .] The Earth is our mother: if you respect it by feeding it with the manure suitable to it, it will reward you. Manure is only the director of an immense orchestra. Its work is spiritual.[6]

The spirituality of manure! One imagines what a writer like Rabelais or Quevedo could do with that metaphor. Waste is fascinating because it can disintegrate indefinitely, lead multiple lives. It is a creature of metamorphoses, like the gods, and like them it is subject to the great cycles of perpetual change. The revolution begins in the toilets! 'José Bové's system of composting toilets greatly impressed Cohn-Bendit,' read an admiring headline in *Le Nouvel Observateur* in 2009![7] Moreover, the Brazilian NGO SOS Atlantic Forest seeks to minimize the water used in toilets by encouraging people to urinate in the shower or in the bathtub. If the whole family adopted this behaviour, we could save twelve litres of water per day per household![8] No more toilet-training for children: don't hold it, let go, it's good for the planet! To defecate is to create. Long live the great regression. The activist webzine *Alternet*, based in San Francisco, proposes, half-ironically, half-seriously, 'pissing ecologically', and 'burning poop' by recycling baby diapers as fuel.[9] Again in California, a French journalist visiting an organic farm reports that:

> I put on rubber boots to take part in the cycle of fertility, in other words, to make compost, the cornerstone of biodynamic farming. I scoop up the horse manure and carry my booty to the fields where we are going to undertake the magic preparation. 'It's like a terrine,' Ryan says: a layer of manure, a layer of earth, a layer of straw, a layer of fresh grass, and so on, and then the whole thing is sprayed with water to make it hold together. Then comes the key step: introducing the biodynamic pellets, strange preparations [. . .] mixed with earth to 'further fertilize the humus', Mike explains. Each child puts his or her pellet in the manure bare-handed. Karina, who has studied literature, urges me to imitate her. 'You'll see, it's warm, it's like putting your hand into Gaia's womb!'[10]

We may be surprised to find Gaia's womb confused with the intestinal system. But these mysteries are beyond us. It is true that with the faecal pyramid we are somewhere between a recipe, an initiatory ritual, and an enema. The epiphany of the excremental is close to redemption: the poetry of the entrails, the lyricism of pestilence, the majesty of rubbish! In the same way of thinking, the craziest ideas flourish – for example, using methane gas to power automatic tellers or paying a firm's employees in vegetables. Ah! Salary increases in leeks and turnips!

For a politics of lightness

Another path proposed by our growth-repentants: lightening the human person. A young New Yorker, Colin Beavan, vowed to reduce his carbon imprint as much as possible while living for a whole year in the heart of Manhattan, with his family, on the ninth floor of an apartment building. He decided to no longer use the elevator, to switch off the air-conditioning and the refrigerator, to give up all kinds of motorized transportation, including the bus and subway, to stop using plastic, to no longer buy products that came from distant countries, and to give up toilet paper. He also tried, not without a sense of humour, to get his wife and child to accept these new rules. 'I didn't just want to reduce my carbon impact. I wanted to have no environmental impact.'[11]

To leave no trace, not to assault the Earth's atmosphere, to arrive at carbon neutrality, to defy weight: a strange ideal of self-effacement. Lightness has its martyrs – anorexics – , its heroes – acrobats, tightrope walkers, and dancers – , and its pious – the proponents of reversing growth, who no longer have faith in existence as it is. The ultimate end of this mentality is the slow extinction of the human race, an invasive species that should be shrunk to the size of a pin. For fear of doing harm, of being in debt, we have to behave like an invisible tribe that emits no signal. With our young New Yorker, we take up residence in the epic of extenuation, in the vertigo of an endless diminution. To reduce one's impact on the planet is not only to deprive oneself for its sake of all the pleasures of life – such as tea, coffee, alcohol – but especially to subject oneself to a daily calculation, never to emerge from the mathematical logic, and to ask oneself breathless questions of this kind: 'In precisely what sense can that [plastic] box of salad on sale at Whole Foods three thousand miles and five days from [where it was grown] truly be said to be organic?'[12]

A simple airplane trip to New England for Thanksgiving gives rise to intense speculations for these young New Yorkers. In the end, it is given up since travelling by plane is the most polluting thing that Beavan thinks his little family could do.[13] Who would have thought that more than a century after Edison the privileged youth of wealthy countries would be dreaming about giving up electricity and pulling the plug, like 57 per cent of Africans,[14] those lucky people who have neither running water nor a reliable energy delivery system. One favoured part of humanity would thus throw itself into voluntary poverty while the other, the more numerous part, enters noisily and enthusiastically into the affluent society? But we cannot escape the infernal universe of consumerism this way. We confirm it a hundred times over. We have simply become alert consumers who can't be taken in and who wonder, regarding any object whatever – a kiwi, a banana, a tub of yogurt: how much does this cost the planet? In fact, we are practising a kind of double labelling, because we add to the price indicated the real price in terms of pollution. (Carbon labelling is also a protectionist measure that penalizes imported products that do not meet its standards.)

The commissars of carbon

On what values do we want to base our life in common? For advocates of ecologism, on a penury shared by all, once 'a norm of sufficiency' (André Gorz) has been established, that is, on an inverted materialism. A permanent critical concern keeps us attached to the commercial sphere. This recalls obsessive people who scrutinize every one of their acts for fear that they might accidentally do something that departs from their ritual. With these maniacal procedures we are far from Rimbaud's insouciance; instead, we have become people who use calculators to subject every purchase to a merciless equation. The moral poverty of mortification! Now we blow our noses ecologically, using every corner of the tissue, we write on both sides of every sheet of paper in order to avoid wasting anything, and we make our own washable diapers, if we can.[15] It has been seriously suggested that we should hand out 'climatic rationing tickets' that would penalize people guilty of going beyond their carbon allotment. Here the amiable verbiage of a few eccentrics could easily turn into fascism if, to our misfortune, they were to come to power. The consumption of water and energy would become a social stigma, with the prize to be given to the most niggardly tightwad. Just imagine new political commissars distinguishing categories of pariahs on the basis of their CO_2 quotas. Woe to bachelors who use twice as much as an individual living in a three-person household. Woe to babies, who should be subject to a supplementary tax of $5,000 as well as an annual tax of $800, according to a professor writing in the *Medical Journal of Australia*. On the other hand, adults who agreed to be sterilized would receive carbon credits. Woe also to the obese and divorced, who put an extra burden on the planet, according to the *New Scientist*. And finally, the Swedish Ministry of Sustainable Development points out that men exhale a much higher amount of carbon dioxide than women do (this is probably a question of hormones; the reason is not given).[16]

Everywhere groups of heretics are emerging who have to be re-educated or regarded as irredeemable; their fate remains to be decided. One can laugh at these classifications, but they would send a shiver down our backs if someday 'a government of ecological liberation', legislating in the name of the planet, decided to save people in spite of themselves. As in the Christian religion, a temptation avoided is equivalent to a good action: witness the notion of 'negawatts', which consists in not making use of energy and thus diminishing 'our daily ration of watts' (Amory Lovins). Or the concept of 'net avoided pollution' invented by the president of Ecuador, Rafael Correa: the point is to avoid development of the oil-producing region of Yasuni National Park, a model of biodiversity, in exchange for international financial compensation, with the goal of someday moving beyond an 'extractivist economy'. But here, too, the virtue of one party presupposes the vice of the majority: a sin not committed is the equivalent of a gift of grace, on the condition that other people, elsewhere, sink into sin. Just as in the days of the USSR there was socialism in only one country, now morals are practised in only one country. In fact, these contradictions affect us all: ideally, we would like to strengthen the protection of nature without giving up the advantages of comfort (in the future, great inventions will win popular approval if they allow us to do both). This is the dilemma of a nation like Norway, an ardent defender of the environment and at the same time a very wealthy oil-producer. It promotes a cause that it also tramples on. Even Germany, which is very proud of its recent anti-nuclear record – it will close all its nuclear power reactors by 2020 – will be forced, while waiting for alternative power-generation technologies to be developed, to buy 'impure' electricity from France and continue to consume highly polluting coal bought in Russia.

Everything has a price, that is the message these rebels send us: we must no longer salt roads in the winter because salt pollutes water tables, and also produces CO_2 because trucks are used to spread it. Cars will smash into trees, people will hole up at home, but at least the soil will not suffer. We have to recycle, reduce, relocalize, patch, repair – all operations that are useful, no doubt, but hardly exhilarating. We constantly oscillate between aggressiveness toward the human race and a generalized naïve altruism: on its cups made of recycled cardboard Starbucks prints this edifying notice: 'This Starbucks paper cup saved more than 100,000 trees last year. [. . .] This cup saves trees by using 10% recycled fiber after use.'

Praise for the negative: all that counts is what one has not done, and a human being's grandeur consists entirely in avoiding and not in accomplishing. But for that very fact everything becomes highly dramatic.

Drinking a glass of water or a cup of tea, eating an apple, immediately evoke images of devastated forests, disembowelled lands, mountains levelled, oceans destroyed. All the Earth's pain cries out to us and we remain deaf, blind, immured in our selfish enjoyment. We wound the planet with each breath we draw: its great, sick body begs us to stop drinking coffee, eating imported exotic fruit, using chemical products, travelling by car, train, or jet planes that tear from the globe's entrails tonnes of petroleum that has matured there for millions of years and is used up in a few hours. We are asked to stay home, to abandon the general wanderlust that has seized our contemporaries.[17] Two centuries after the railway began to open up the countryside, to connect people, the splendours of enclosure and sedentariness are being sung again. What used to be forced on us by poverty and custom is now recommended by our mother Gaia. This is the end of a cycle that began with the Renaissance and that proclaimed the abolition of boundaries and shackles, the retreat of borderlines: now we have to return to the closed spaces of the Middle Ages, idolize our street, our town, remain bound to the place where we were born.

But even those who advocate the prohibition or limitation of travelling, which would be subjected, as in the former communist countries, to a kind of poll tax, spend their time in aeroplanes, moving from one convention to another and trying to be present everywhere on Earth to preach the Good Word. The two figures in the movement who are most prominent in the French media, Nicolas Hulot and Yann Arthus-Bertrand, travel by jet and helicopter so frequently that the latter has been called the inventor of 'helicology' (Paul Ariès).

What should we conclude from these pious exhortations? That we cannot allow a minority of Green autocrats to decide for us whether or not renunciation is important. We are going through a crisis in ways of life that makes change imperative. Catastrophe is never anything but a big word for change. It is both a misfortune and a denouement, a tragedy and a transition. The anxiety of our time is the anxiety of transformation, the breakdown of an order that is decomposing without our knowing what will follow it. Nevertheless, how can we fail to be struck by the mediocrity of the paths proposed, which limit themselves to recycling the old ideal of penitence, which returns under the mask of the nice. If we have to limit ourselves, lower our consumption, let that be the subject of a great debate, or even a referendum as major as that on ending the use of nuclear power. Since the first oil crisis in 1973, our fellow citizens have shown that they are capable of making a virtue of necessity. Today, the proponents of ecologism are in the situation of the workers' movement at the end of the nineteenth century, divided into libertarian, democratic, and totalitarian tendencies. If the latter wins out because of a crisis or blackmail, if the extremists drown out the moderates, the new sobriety will have the bitter taste of concentration camps and prisons. In the wrong hands, the best of causes can degenerate into an abomination. That is the great lesson taught by the twentieth century.

Robinson Crusoe, or the World Turned into a Desert

We are all Robinson Crusoes; we have all been shipwrecked by the cosmos and cannot hope to be saved by anyone. For us as for Crusoe, life consists in living in a hostile environment. Hardly have the waves cast Daniel Defoe's hero on the shores of a luxuriant island off the mouth of the Orinoco before he hastens to recuperate from the wreckage of his ship what he needs to subsist. He draws from it 'the biggest Magazine of all Kinds [. . .] that ever were laid up, I believe, for one Man'.[18] From the carpenter's toolbox he takes all the tools necessary for sawing, planing, and planting, as well as gunpowder, muskets, rifles, a telescope, a spade, a hoe, and a shovel, along with needles and thread and two cats and a dog. A clumsy handyman, by turns a mason, farmer, basket-maker, potter, and baker, Crusoe is an unworthy heir and vegetates in an extremely precarious situation. The slightest oversight could prove fatal; he wastes nothing and limits his needs as much as he can. Against the unpredictable turbulence of the ocean and the savagery of nature, he constructs a world of order and reason, plants wheat, domesticates a herd of goats, and builds two dwellings. He has been made (by Joyce and Coetzee) the symbol of British conquest and a spokesman for colonization. To do so is to forget that Crusoe is a transgressor, an irregular. He has committed the supreme crime: not being content with the mediocre life that his father intended for him, yielding to his vagabond impulses and the call of the sea.

After ten years, once he has acquired his comfort, he reigns like a pasha over this cordial jungle that he has put straight. But 'banished from human society', he suffers from loneliness, even though he has trained a parrot to call him by name. The tropical idyll is not enough for him. Nature tamed ought to be only the prelude to bonds with his fellow humans. A footprint on the beach plunges him into throes of terror and hope: he is afraid of being eaten by cannibals or taken prisoner by the Spanish, the quartermasters of the Inquisition. The encounter with Friday, whom he saves from being devoured by cannibals, transfigures him, even though he makes Friday his servant, and though Friday is often more ingenious than his master and perhaps becomes his lover (as moderns with

perverted minds, that is how we can interpret him).
Robinson's life turns into bliss.

Michel Tournier, in his magnificent sequel to this
story,[19] makes the island the place where Crusoe
de-civilizes himself, grows unaccustomed to
himself, to the point that he casts his semen in a
rose-coloured combe to become a seed caught in
the massive flesh of the archipelago. Friday is no
longer the docile servant but the tempter who
makes his master a savage again, pushes him along
the path of a solar eroticism, of a close communion
with the elements.

The island, cast in the middle of the seas as the
Earth is on the limits of the galaxies, is a metaphor
of the social contract, a first dawn of the world.
To be shipwrecked on the shores of an unknown
land is to begin over, in a few months or years, the
whole human adventure, to start anew from zero.
This is as in the American television series *Lost*, in
which the survivors of a plane crash are stranded
on an atoll with mysterious powers (the influence
of Jules Verne is obvious), and realize that in their
former lives they had already gone astray and will
no longer be able to readapt themselves to the
civilized world. The island depopulates the universe, hands it over to telluric forces alone. If a
robinsonnade is a world without others (Gilles
Deleuze),[20] it is a mistake to impute this characteristic to Robinson Crusoe. To the idle question:
'What book would you take with you to a desert
island?' he seems to reply: no book, but rather the
company of a human being. This hirsute being clad
in a nanny-goat's pelt and sporting a grotesque hat
was, in his own way, more civilized than we are.

9

The Noble Savage in the Lucerne

What is speed? A *strophe* in search of its *cata*.
Saint-Pol Roux

In 1970, there appeared in *Politique Hebdo* and then in *Charlie Mensuel* a cartoon strip by Gébé headed: *We stop everything, we reflect, and it's not sad*. It was the *Year 01*, the chronicle of a world of happy idleness, without work or markets, where the siesta and free love reigned supreme. All services are absent except for the most essential – water, electricity, food supply. It was in this strip that the theme of a libertarian ecology first appeared, in a form very far from the sectarianism it has since acquired. This velvet insurrection arose from revulsion at the rows of post-war apartment buildings that produced an unparalleled disfiguration of the world. (It is too often forgotten that the 1960s and 1970s were also a time when a general aesthetic crime was committed, of which Le Corbusier, that brilliant incarcerator of humanity, was one of the prototypes.)

The desire to stop everything, breathe, take a break: that was a symptom of an inverted messianic hope. Time had to be suspended, and the disastrous error that had caused the European world to slip into an unreasonable busyness had to be corrected. The great ecstasy of interruption. In their agitation, the rich countries suspected that something essential had been lost and that it was up to them to rediscover it. The Third World has long been a place of possible regeneration for ardent souls. But when it doesn't sink into dictatorship, it becomes infected, especially in Asia, by the commercial and industrial disease. The pilgrimage back to the sources will have to take two other paths: either re-create Eden within the heart of the Hell that is civilization, through a simulacrum of rural life, or seek out pre-lapsarian primitive worlds where 'humanity's sources in childhood' (Paul Gaugin) can be found.

The golden age rediscovered

We have to 'return to the Upper Paleolithic, or at least the early Iron Age', we are told by North American neo-primitivists who are certain that the only way to rehabilitate humanity is to return to a society of hunter-gatherers. Henceforth we must take into account not only the 'scant two hundred years of revolutionary history' that have preceded us, but all the civilizations that have succeeded one another since the dawn of humanity, in order to appropriate what is best in them.[1] At the very time when we are being urged to abandon consumer society, we are subjected to the philosophy of the smorgasbord or, more precisely, of anthropological picking and choosing. For instance, in Philip José Farmer's science fiction series *Riverworld* (1971–83), in which a party that includes a Neanderthal man, the English explorer Richard Burton and Hermann Goering travels back up the endless river of universal history, visiting one by one all the cultures that have ever existed, without ever reaching the river's source. In the eyes of their advocates, the first peoples are admirable because they use carbon sparingly, respect the cycle of the seasons, and are less inegalitarian than we are. In addition, they have the advantage of clustering in small groups of individuals who know each other and are never submerged in the anonymous multitude. Natural man, Rousseau already told us, had a robust constitution, was far-sighted, and had no need for remedies and still less for doctors.[2] The savage, modern writers were to repeat, is his own leader, and practises gender equality; he works little, enjoys an unheard-of abundance (Marshall Sahlins), picks fruit off trees like customers in a supermarket, and above all suffers from neither the stress nor the insecurity of modern peoples.[3]

This neo-nativism runs through a whole protest literature ranging from works by the Nobel Prize winner Jean-Marie Gustave Le Clézio to various alternative anthropologies and other subaltern studies.[4] The savage is the sage we urgently need to avoid sinking into the abyss: he escapes the twofold disaster constituted by the Industrial Revolution and over-population, he cares nothing for the technological boom, and seems backward only because he is ahead of us. Through his indifference to our civilization, his stubborn refusal to adopt our work rhythms and our stultifying leisure activities, he demonstrates the dead end into which we have wandered. To follow his example is not to wage a regressive battle but rather to be in the van of a major change: '[W]e are fighting a rearguard action, but paradoxically this battle is a battle for the future. When an army is headed toward a dead end, sooner or later it has to turn around, and then the rearguard becomes the vanguard.'[5] In short, from the point of view of a 'moderate reversal of growth', progressivism today means returning to the past in order to draw from it lessons in discernment and moderation.

The Kapauku people of Papua-New Guinea devote no more than two hours a day to subsistence agriculture.

The same is true of the Kuikuru Indians in the Amazon Basin and Russian peasants before the October revolution. [. . .] [D]idn't these groups sense that an increase in the time spent on agricultural work would produce only a marginal additional yield?[6]

A curious reflex: an ingenuity is projected onto these distant peoples that is the opposite of our own beliefs. They do not exist in themselves, in their singularity: their value consists solely in the fact that they are not like us, which is the most ethnocentric way of considering them (although choosing as an example the Russian moujik, who was subject to forced labour and oppressed – serfdom was not abolished until 1861 – implies a strange conception of history). It is one thing to seek to protect 'primitive peoples' from the greed of promoters, gold-diggers, and the zeal of missionaries, and another to adopt them as models at the risk of falling into the folklore of the noble savage. These tiny nations are thus said to have understood that excess productivity would bring them nothing but unhappiness and rivalry. They foresaw all the sorrows that the culture of yield and profit provokes in developed societies.

But isn't this to fall into a retrospective illusion, to see them with our industrial mentality? These peoples testify to a pleasantness of life, to a purity that was destroyed, for example, by the catastrophe of the *Conquista* in Latin America without reducing our nostalgia for it. They are still connected with us negatively; they constitute our exact opposite. Consider an advertisement that appeared in the *New York Times Magazine*[7] and shows a young American Indian woman 'raised on wild rice and sustainability': 'Think Indian! To think Indian is to make eco-buildings with spruce roots or rebar. Help tribal college students preserve their way of thinking.' On the pretext of preserving a way of life, isn't this a way of projecting onto the last North American tribes our own concerns about pollution? The

Indian of the Amazon, the Aborigine of Australia, and the Inuit of the Far North possess all the qualities we lack. They are still connected with the great forces of Nature, they know that each tree incarnates a divinity, they practise 'the sharing of wealth [. . .] medical care based on incantation or on plants'.[8] They respect life whereas we trample on it, they inhabit a time that is mythical as much as it is real, and are still supported by an oral tradition that we have lost. But above all they warn us about 'the imminence of the final destruction of the world' (Jean-Marie Gustave Le Clézio). Having themselves been hunted down, scattered, and destroyed, they know about cataclysms and can sense collapse. The primitive is the perfect combination of frugality, wisdom, and concord. Whereas our culture floods the planet with its triviality and produces nothing but hovels, slums, and dumps, in their resistance to our civilization natives round the world have much to teach us.

Only being initiated by a shaman, sojourning under a yurt, or escaping to live among the globe's last tribes can procure for us a feeling of salvation, tear us away from this world in the grip of a narrow rationalism.

> Today, encountering the Indian world is no longer a luxury; it has become a necessity for anyone who wants to understand what is happening in the modern world. But it is not just about understanding; it is about trying to go all the way to the end of all the dark corridors, trying to open a few doors: that is, ultimately, trying to survive.[9]

These fragile groups are a metaphor for our vulnerability. Beneath their apparent detachment, they demonstrate that we have gone astray. Endowed with secret, sacred knowledge, they offer us the image of an innocence that only a flashback of the human adventure might allow us to rediscover. To follow them is to learn from them, to recharge one's batteries in a primordial time in which humans and nature were not dissociated but still maintained a relationship of complicity and empathy. That is how we can explain the media success of someone like Raoni, the chief of the Kayapos in Brazil, with his elaborate headdress and his lower lip deformed by a wooden disc that gives his mouth the shape of an ashtray or bowl (this is the traditional attribute of warriors, and is intended to frighten their adversaries). Having become famous throughout the world for his opposition to the deforestation of the Amazon region and the construction of the Belo Monte bridge in the state of Para, he has been received by all the great personages of this world: the Pope, François Mitterrand, Prince Charles, and King Juan Carlos, as well as Jacques Chirac, who wrote the preface to one of his books. Invited to the Cannes Film Festival in 2010, along with Mathieu Amalric, photographed with Nicolas Hulot, this 'guardian of the eco-citizen's conscience' seems likely to become for the defence of the planet what the Dalai Lama was for post-Christian spirituality in the West.

But it is one thing to protect cultures that are disappearing or vacillating, and another to seek in them the answer to our problems, or, worse yet, to imitate them in order to become the Last of the Mohicans, a white witness to a human community that has been annihilated. The shaman, the witch-doctor, and the bard become our professors of authenticity, regenerating elements for an exhausted civilization. The passionate defence of inaugural societies is never more than a way of judging ourselves through them. Whereas during the colonial period we decried their backwardness, now we marvel at their miraculous equilibrium, but the procedure is the same: the presupposition is still the Western mode of life, which is now denigrated. To extol the wisdom of the Iroquois or the Navajos, the generosity of the Melanesians, or the moderation of the Aborigines is still to see them through our lacks and difficulties, to posit them as exemplary counter-values opposed to the world in which we live. Let us leave aside the fact that so far as they are concerned, this involves a phantasmatic reconstruction. The ecological 'purity' of the first peoples is, as we have seen, an environmentalist myth forged in departments of anthropology; like us, these peoples have also practised massive deforestation on their own scale and contributed to the extinction of a number of species. Our Edenic predecessors were already ravagers, but with limited means.[10]

Behind the colourful fabric of rites and customs, it is still our own obsessions that we are projecting onto these 'natural' peoples, who thus become spokesmen for our fears and impasses. They are pure ideas that we oppose to over-population, degradation, the market. We can seek them in humanity's past or in its near future. Consider James Cameron's film *Avatar* (2009), which bears witness to this ecological alternate history. It recounts the invasion of the planet Pandora, in 2154, by an army of Earthmen – Americans, naturally – who have come there in search of a magic mineral ore whose possession would allow them to cope with their energy crisis. Pandora is inhabited by a race of supermen with blue skins, half Smurfs, half Tarzans, the Na'vis, who are three metres tall and live in a luxuriant forest full of monsters and dragons in a luminescent organic milieu. War breaks out between the invaders and the natives. The latter are first defeated, but then triumph with the help of thousands of animals (including titanosaurs resembling mega-rhinoceroses) that kick the GIs out of Pandora. The Earthmen, incarnated by nasty, over-armed cowboys, are guilty twice over, both of crushing peoples and of violating Nature out of cupidity. *Avatar*'s enormous success, which was comparable to that of Kevin Costner's *Dances with Wolves* (1990), proceeded from this confluence between an anti-imperialist fable and an ecological allegory. The cause of the planet and that of enslaved cultures is one and the same.[11]

We have to cultivate our gardens

The same quest for authenticity makes so many alternative movements seek to re-evaluate the agricultural world. Whereas in Europe the peasant has become a guardian of the countryside, but also an entrepreneur in the van of modernity whose management of input and output is entirely computerized, we are here asked to cultivate our gardens in the city. We are supposed to blanket urban areas with vegetable gardens, grow lettuce, tomatoes, and radishes on our balconies, raise chickens and rabbits at home. Urban gardeners will come to teach you the rudiments of the craft, initiate you into the mysteries of sowing seeds, hoeing, and watering. A return of the august figure of the sower amid the concrete, a rehabilitation of market gardening as it used to be practised in workers' gardens on the outskirts of towns. To reconcile the city and the countryside is to counterbalance asphyxia with oxygen and the monotony of stone with the diversity of plants, to make up for the gallop of overwork with the gentle trot of germination and maturation. The ideal of the urban garden is not new: it goes back to the seventeenth century at least, when it was promoted by aristocrats who planted trees, groves, and shrubs in order to create solitary spaces amid crowds and bustle.[12] The cold geometry of avenues was broken by bridle-paths, curtains of greenery, rows of lime and plane trees; surprise was mixed with pleasure, visual enchantment with sweet fragrances. What a contrast, in this regard, between London, Amsterdam, or Berlin, which were covered with vast parks, and Paris, which had reduced its green spaces to a minimum! Moreover, the garden has a civilizing effect: the flower beds reflect the moral value of their owners. Caring for one's roses, hydrangeas, and lawns, producing thick, luscious grass, is also a way of competing with one's neighbours, asserting one's personality.

Today, city-dwellers sponsor organic farms near large metropolises that provide them with fruit and vegetables, eliminate intermediaries, and combine freshness with proximity. The *tekei* in Japan, the food guilds in Switzerland, and the Amap (Association for the Maintenance of Peasant Agriculture) in France have instituted contracts between buyers and producers that do away with middlemen. These contracts guarantee on a weekly basis and at a reasonable price produce that has been grown without pesticides or chemical inputs. In the United States, the 'Greenthusiasts' movement, which is said to have included more than thirty million persons in 2007, brings together people who are looking for a healthy and sustainable lifestyle, or LOHAS (Lifestyle of Health and Sustainability).[13] In Germany, activists recommend a vast, food-producing greenbelt around metropolises whose breadth would correspond to 'a day's ride on horseback (25 kilometres)', this detail emphasizing the desire to return to a period before motor vehicles.[14] In opposition to supermarkets and expensive imports from abroad, in France we are asked to rediscover the virtues of cabbage from Pontoise, asparagus from Argenteuil, chickens from Houdan, and dandelions from Montmagny. When will we be eating foods produced within the city – tomatoes from Plaine Monceau, beans from Butte-Aux-Cailles, squash from Saint-Germain-des-Prés, honey from Mouffetard, organic marijuana from Montmartre, and salsify from Belleville? The city-dweller is expected to become a horticulturist, a nurseryman, and a market gardener, to combine convivially gentle techniques, domestic livestock, and food production. 'Green guerrilleros', pacifists who drop little vegetal bombs on fallow land, are seeding empty lots and abandoned railway lines. No particular talent is required, just good will and courage: in New York there is even an Incompetent Gardeners' Association! The same ambition drives 'slow cities' concerned to limit their size by highlighting the local and 'bio-regions'. A whole neo-potager utopia is being set up that seeks to combine respect for seasonal rhythms with control over the food supply, excluding any manipulation by the food industry – at least until large distributors co-opt these networks and make rebellion against its hold on this domain a vector of its extension. The great ruse of Green capitalism consists in thriving on challenges to its control.

Dismantling the asphalt carcass of large cities by making them green, constructing suspended forests, vertical copses, covering our streets, avenues, and squares with trees and grass, filling our courtyards with goats and cocks, our roofs with beehives, and so on, is not a 1970s-style return to the earth, a long-haired exile in some remote region like Lozère or Ardèche, but instead a return to one's own bit of land, even if it is the size of a postage stamp. The goal of this apartment countryside is also to put an end to the division of labour that is a dispossession, to reconstruct a whole individual capable of producing his or her own means of subsistence. Whereas cereal growers and livestock raisers are suspected of raping the soil, the new 'urban farmer' is motivated by scruples, slowness, and the spirit of autonomy. Asked what human beings' ethical stance with regard to the earth should be, Jean-Marie Pelt replies:

> I imagine something rather like gardening. And I imagine something like it in a world in which people treat twenty hectares at once in order to grow wheat. One is the exact opposite of the other. A person who cultivates a hundred hectares of wheat is called a grower (*exploitant*) but in fact he is an exploiter (*exploiteur*) [. . .] the gardener has a whole humble practice of the earth. He is close to the earth that he loves.[15]

Let us cultivate our gardens in order to restore flavour to our food and protect ourselves against uncontrollable variations in supply. But these islands of purity set up in opposition to the corruption of the world seem to be animated more by an ideal of retreat than by a desire to discover new things. Here as elsewhere, the spirit of retraction has supplanted the spirit of expansion. Planting our own cabbages, baking our own bread, adorning our cities with flowers, what could be more noble? Can that quench the infinite thirst of younger generations? Can it put a stop to the current degradation, overcome planetary processes that go beyond us?

Humankind diminished or humankind expanded

What is striking since the end of communism is the poverty of the alternatives opposed to the system, as if 1989 had dried up utopia. We endlessly recycle the debris of the socialist and anarchist projects because we are unable to recover their energy. In the nineteenth and twentieth centuries, political and artistic minorities had shown an ability to enrich collective aspirations, to draw people toward an increasing joy and well-being. Today they are, at least in Europe, the apostles of slandering the world as it is. We are living in the time of regressive avant-gardes: instead of inventing, they denigrate. And ecologism adds to this general resentment a questionable scientific guarantee.

For example, how strange is the furious opposition to consumer society, which seems to be shared by everyone! Instead of being outraged by poverty, we are offended by the comforts we enjoy. Consumerism scandalizes people because it reveals the simple structure of desire, which wants the satisfaction of appetites as well as their renewal. It spares us the painful, twofold experience of frustration and satiety: always satisfied, always kept ready for more by the abundance of possible objects. Its genius and its curse is its ability to make the superfluous seem indispensable. But civilization is nothing but the exponential increase of desires that expand our souls and our horizons. It is a 'miserable miracle', perhaps, but it is so powerful that it is irrefutable and is approved throughout the world. In the name of what can we deny commercialized enchantment to peoples who are deprived of it, forbid them to have flat screens or mobile phones, especially since some great department stores, some display windows, are collective creations of great beauty? Let us recall the abject reaction of West German progressives – who were privileged bourgeois – when the Berlin Wall came down in 1989: they compared their future compatriots from the GDR, who rushed in to take advantage of food and clothing shops, to monkeys rushing to eat bananas and oranges. Our lofty intellectuals who today hold their noses when confronted by emergent countries are behaving toward Indians, Chinese, and Brazilians the way Marie-Antoinette behaved with regard to the starving during the French Revolution ('Let them eat cake!'). How can 'frugal abundance' (J.-B. Foucauld) compete with such a powerful system of desire communicated by the media, advertising, and fashion? What we have to work on is the multiplication of pleasures and passions, not their extinction.

One may find supermarkets depressing, and think pathetic those customers who behave, during sales, like pillagers eager to get their part of the booty. But no one expects shopping to give meaning to his or her life. The discourse about the emptiness of consumerism is as empty as what it denounces, and the silliness of the detractors is equalled only by that of the adulators. We can go even further: the objects that surround us have souls, whether we like it or not. Cars, mobile phones, screens, and clothes are in every respect not gadgets but rather enlargements of ourselves. They would not elicit such infatuation if they were not inhabited by us as we are inhabited by them. By expanding the range of the possible, they offer us a certain autonomy. These marvellous tools free us from time and space, allow us to act, speak, and communicate over thousands of kilometres, give us access to abilities that used to be attributed solely to magicians and sorcerers: ubiquity, teleportation. They are supplementary organs grafted onto our bodies. Human beings produce tools but are also the product of their tools, of the artifices they have developed and that strengthen them.

Better yet: luxury and refinement are indispensable for the blossoming of any great civilization. We must demand, of course, long-lasting equipment that consumes little carbon, light bulbs that do not explode after a few weeks, refrigerators as sturdy as tanks, and batteries that last. But nothing would be sadder than objects that lasted forever and would thus deprive us of the frenzy of shopping and spare us the mad seductiveness of novelty. Hence there is nothing strictly material that does not also have psychic resonances, and familiar objects are spiritual objects in waiting, available spirit. Contrary to the anathemas pronounced by people like Heidegger, technology has become a second nature, an extension of our nervous systems, and this phenomenon will grow further with the grafting – already possible – of implants and microprocessors in the body in order to make up for failing functions and repair cells, and with the introduction of 'living neurons' in our computers. Artifice is our second or third skin, as indispensable as the first. The future human being will be prosthetic or will not be at all.

How can one not be dazzled by the beauty of an aeroplane's fuselage, a graceful airport arch, a soaring skyscraper, or the elegance of a computer screen? Tocqueville was wrong to decry the passion for well-being that allegedly distracts our fellow citizens from political concerns: the material environment is not simply futile but supports self-fulfilment. Modern conveniences permit us to construct ourselves without exhausting our strength, without having to struggle and fight to seek our pittance, to hunt game, to sew our clothes. Thus we can devote our energy to something other than the simple survival to which a whole school of denunciation would like to confine us. To put the point in Marxist terms, modern technology makes possible a broader reproduction instead of the simple reproduction to which the proletarian wage-slave was doomed. Among other things, poverty is the reduction of everyone to his or her elementary needs: food, clothing, movement, lodging; it is the impossibility of living without counting. Peoples always revolt because they have too little, only rarely because they have too much. No one has ever seen millionaires marching in the streets shouting: Wealth, that's enough! Enough designer suits, luxury cars, palaces, and gold watches!

Can humanity fulfil itself by following paths other than material success? This question, raised for example by George Steiner castigating 'the sterile cruelty of wealth', is profoundly idle: both are required, mind and matter together. One part of humanity has tasted the fruits of comfort; to suddenly deprive it of them to realize a hypothetical cultural elevation is very naïve; we would have penury plus a lack of culture. With ecologism, the UN's definition of security – 'freedom from need and fear' – would be inverted: the minimum necessary for life and dread. Who, moreover, is to decide which needs are legitimate and which futile? To oppose goods to social ties, in accord with the fashionable cliché, is to forget that the former have never prevented the latter, on the contrary: Christmas gifts, even if they sometimes sink to the level of a commercial orgy, are also a way of strengthening familial and conjugal bonds, of showing affection. To give is always to declare an attachment, on condition that the other not be humiliated by a present that is too sumptuous or too mean. In all societies, relations between people pass through objects that receive from them an emotive quality and even a rare intensity.

We play several roles at once – workers, purchasers of services, citizens of a nation, individuals concerned about self-fulfilment – and we have to play each of these roles without sacrificing any of them. Consumerism remains an incontestable advance to the extent that it limits itself to its own functions and does not claim to govern, by its logic alone, all problems – education, politics, culture. Therefore we have constantly to renegotiate the lines of demarcation separating the commercial from the non-commercial, and not auction off to the highest bidder the symbolic territories constituted by the schools, the judicial system, healthcare, and nature.

We can distinguish three ages in our relationship to nature since the seventeenth century: the age of scarcity for a majority of the population, which lasted up to the middle of the twentieth century; the age of gluttony, with the invention of credit (which reached its apogee in the subprime crisis that occurred in the United States in 2008); and finally the age of duly considered desires, into which we may now be entering, and which will cause us to move from a property economy to a rental economy. Why should we tolerate the costly possession of objects that can be rented and returned at will, a car for instance? Purchasing, with its simple rules and obvious pleasures, will persist because it procures all the joys of an unlimited supply and an intense hunger immediately satisfied. It is better to democratize consumption than to abolish it; the real scandal is not to be able to participate in it for lack of means. In any case, money, Seneca already pointed out, is one of the preferables, along with health, no matter what destiny one chooses for oneself. Every way of life is an affirmation of values and ideas. A civilized society does not scorn material goods but offers several definitions of wealth, financial, moral, and spiritual, and does not reject any of them. It is one thing for everyone to reorganize the hierarchy between the essential and the accessory, to redeal the cards in relation to his or her imperatives, but every life has value only through the portion of poetry and splendour that it brings out and that alone gives it value. In the United States, the counterweight to commercial frenzy resides in patriotism and religious faith, the two things that democratic empire holds sacred. In Europe, it resides in culture understood as a common treasure and power of creation, in studious idleness, in the art of living and living well with others. Perhaps the Old World is better adapted to change than the New, to the extent that its ideal of competition is less ferocious, the cult of work less frenetic, and the ability to rediscover slowness and sweetness – that is, new uses of time, new intoxications with the minuscule – more firmly anchored.

A fear of movement

The contemporary challenge, which it may be impossible to meet, is the following: not renouncing any of the advantages of development and at the same time not suffering from the collateral damage it does. Promoting a decent life for seven billion people without exhausting the planet's resources. Finding a source of clean and reliable energy that can be stored up, whether it is solar, nuclear, hydroelectric, geothermic, tidal, or other. At a time when wind power and solar power remain embryonic and the demand for energy has never been so strong, it is irresponsible to ask us immediately to give up petroleum, atomic power, gas, bituminous schists, and coal, on the pretext that they are dangerous and polluting. It is not clear that nuclear power is finished, despite the proclamations of its detractors, who are only too glad to present it as an obsolete technology. It is likely that for the immediate future we will continue to use a variety of energy sources, including even the most archaic ones, until a better solution is achieved. Finally, it is possible that massive investments in innovative technologies will enable humanity to make an exponential leap forward in the next thirty years that will make current debates null and void. Economizing, trimming, tightening belts are merely short-term objectives. Development is both indispensable and potentially destructive if it is extended as such to the human race as a whole. That is the enormous challenge facing us: we have to avoid limiting human progress even as we diminish its costs.

Europeans have never been so concerned about the future as they have been since they stopped believing in it. They mention it in order to keep it at bay and to confine themselves to the anxiety regarding the present. The Old World is experiencing a pandemic of weariness or, to use Spinoza's expression, a preponderance of sad passions. In opposition to defeatism, we could make a list of the good news we've had over the past twenty years: the Arab world is beginning its long and chaotic revolution; democracy is slowly progressing; India, China, Brazil, and South Africa are becoming dominant powers; almost a billion people have emerged from absolute poverty; longevity is increasing in most countries – in China alone, it has increased by thirty-eight years;[16] wars are becoming less frequent;[17] and a number of serious diseases have been eradicated, most recently cattle plague (rinderpest). We have just lived through one of the most prosperous and least violent decades in history, which we nonetheless describe as an abomination. Our perception is inversely proportional to reality. Non-European peoples have become masters of their own destiny, that is the great novelty of our time: they have ceased to revolve around us, to regard us as infallible models. They are developing on the basis of their own traditions, not ours. This is a fascinating paradox: the triumph of Western values, the market economy,

and democracy go hand in hand with the marginaliza-
tion of Europe and America as leading civilizations, as
they collapse under their deficits. This is the end of four
centuries of hegemony, a shift in the centre of gravity
from the West to the East. All that is known. Even the
United States is no longer the ebullient Rome from
which people expect new ideas, eccentric fashions, stupefying initiatives. Bogged down in endless wars, ruined
by an irresponsible politics, having given up the conquest of space, constantly rehearsing its fundamental
neuroses – religious bigotry, distrust of the government,
retrograde puritanism – the United States resembles a
wounded giant brooding on his fall even though he
might someday rise again, and sooner than we think.
For decades, the right and left have urged the advance
of democracy in developing countries. For some, free
markets and privatization are the miraculous remedy;
for others, armed struggle and collectivization are the
only way to liberate people from colonial humiliation.
These counsels have been followed in part, but not at
all as we expected. Economic liberals are vexed to find
nipping at their heels the wretches they thought doomed
to produce inferior imitations and who, like China, are
now innovating and inventing and hold in their hands
Uncle Sam's enormous debt. Those who idolize the
Third World are outraged to see the masses effusively
embrace the spell of the market and consumption. Not
to mention Green activists who are furious to see Asians,
Africans, and South Americans adding to the planet's
carbon debt. Developing countries are guilty of having
escaped their stereotypes: they are not only catching up
with us, but also supplanting us, sparing themselves
decades of laborious research by adopting the most
advanced technological revolutions (witness the success
of the mobile phone in Africa, which has made it possible to dispense with a traditional telephone system).
Unlikely collisions are overturning our mental schemas,
while in Beijing the most unbridled capitalism co-exists

with communist authoritarianism, and in India, formerly a caste society, parliamentary democracy is being
confirmed, thus making this great power better able to
cope with crises than its Marxist neighbour.

The end of condescending or compassionate discourse: everywhere, these young nations have found the
path to their own emancipation at the expense of their
self-proclaimed saviours, everywhere the remedies proposed by the neo-liberals, the idolizers of the Third
World, and the alter-globalists have failed. And ecologism is in real danger of slipping into polite indifference.
Several billion people expect growth and an improvement of their lot. In the name of what could we dare
deny it to them? The best way to cope with the degradation of the environment is first of all the material enrich-
ment of the masses. One has to have access to abundance
to combat evils, and we have to work at the same time
on development and corrections of development. The
new Green puritanism may be nothing other than a
reaction on the part of an irked West, the last avatar of
a despondent neo-colonialism preaching to other cultures a wisdom it has itself never practised. Inundated
to the point of nausea with alarmist prognostications,
we forget that the crisis of capitalism is not worldwide
but Western, that what we are experiencing is not the
end of time but the end of the supremacy of Europe and
the United States over the rest of the globe. While we
pout, the Chinese, Indians, South Africans, and Brazilians are drinking to their resurrection, even if it is fragile.
'Old men like to offer good advice in order to console
themselves for no longer being in a position to give bad
examples' (La Rochefoucauld). European left-wing
movements have already trampled on their principles
twice: first, by confusing education and entertainment,
thus participating in the collapse of the schools; and,
second, by abandoning the battle for equality in favour
of the battle for identity politics, to the point of forgetting the question of social justice and letting the

proletariat drift toward the extreme right. If they now desert the idea of progress, which was the armature of their whole combat, they will no longer have any *raison d'être*. This is probably the first time in contemporary history that a movement claiming to belong to this camp, political ecologism, has proposed to take humanity backward, claiming the guarantee of nature and the cosmos. But time never returns to its source. If our old nations die of fear, morbidity will break them up. To change directions, we will first have to change our fear, that is, our priorities, and rid ourselves of our obsession with defeat. *Environmental concern is universal, but the disease of the end of the world is purely Western.*

Immortality, Up to What Age?

The extension of longevity is a marvellous achievement of medicine, and it adds a temporal depth to lives that used to enter their twilight at the age of thirty or forty. What is more wonderful than to grant ourselves an intoxicating supplement, to still be living and desiring at an age when our ancestors were slowly sinking into their graves? There are several lives in an individual's life, years have ceased to be a verdict, and the die is never cast. Nonetheless, the ideal would be to grow up without ever growing old, to retain to the end the vigour and elasticity one has at the age of thirty, and to die, as it were, in good health. Octogenarians would skip rope, pursue torrid relationships with the young, and the age gap would no longer be shocking because everyone would seem to be the same age.

It is possible to foresee beings with micro-electronic prostheses implanted in their brains, with nano-capsules capable of cleaning their blood, and with night vision, who could live to be a hundred and fifty years old. It is not old age but youth that would have to be prolonged to the end.

Instead, our developed societies resemble retirement homes in which our elders fall victim to all the diseases of old age: cancer, Parkinson's, Alzheimer's. Dependency, infirmity, and senility are nightmares engendered by progress. Soon all humanity will have the same problem because there will be, after the peak of nine billion inhabitants predicted for 2030, a drastic population decrease. We are headed toward a world of old people that will be led by a small elite of striplings.

As for immortality – which is, for the moment, a mere hypothesis – it is not necessarily a cheering prospect. In *Gulliver's Travels*, Swift shows us his hero's encounter with a nation of immortals, the Struldbruggs; they are all very lonely and very unhappy. The utopia of augmented humans endowed with an incredible longevity inverts the order of priorities: the repair of cells and tissues, the reconstruction of molecules as if they were Lego bricks, threatens to absorb all our energy and distract our attention from the real question: what are we to do with our lives? What are we to do with this allocation of additional years if we already don't know what to do with the ones we have? Trying to prolong our lives by any means – giving up tobacco, alcohol, good food, and sex – amounts to forbidding ourselves to live in order to survive beyond a hundred at all costs; to die, as it were, from trying to be immortal. Can one imagine a humanity consisting of centenarians in which sons, grandsons, fathers, grandfathers, and ancestors would be equally hoary, wrinkled, bent, and senile, each incarnating one step along the long road to decrepitude? Every family would cover the spectrum of a century, at least. The great religious question used to be: is there a life after death? For secular societies, the great question is the inverse: is there a life before death? Have we loved, expended, given, embraced enough? Life is not an endurance race in which one has to go on as long as possible, but a certain quality of bonds, emotions, engagements. When it is reduced to a simple churning of our organs, does it still have any value at all? What is sadder than these retirement homes filled with old people abandoned by everyone, waiting for the end, with nothing to do, ruminating their memories and their bitterness, and who are dressed, washed, and fed like scruffy, mumbling infants? Whether one wants to slow time down or accelerate it, something has to take place in a human being's heart that is overwhelming, unexpected. Real life consists in intensity, not in duration. So long as one loves, studies, is astonished, one is immortal right up to one's last day.

Epilogue

The Remedy is Found in the Disease

Either the lugubrious prophets are right that we are rushing toward the abyss and the only avenue left is the human race's voluntary or involuntary self-extinction, or there is still room for manoeuvre, and we should explore it fearlessly. The ecology of disaster is primarily a disaster for ecology: it employs such an outrageous rhetoric that it discourages the best of wills. It tries so hard to avoid our ruin that it will hasten it if we follow its recommendations and wrap the planet in cellophane like a Christo sculpture (we know that in the Swiss and Austrian Alps some ski resorts have covered glaciers with isothermic blankets to keep them from melting). Either ecology persists in imprecations and sterile gestures or it returns in a lucid way to the great idea of humanity's moral progress, learning from its earlier mistakes. A race has begun between the forces of despair and those of human ingenuity.

In other words, the remedy is found in the disease (Jean Starobinski), in the despised industrial civilization, the frightening science, the endless crisis, the globalization that exceeds our grasp: only an increase in research, an explosion of creativity, or an unprecedented technological advance will be able to save us. We have to try to push back the boundaries of the possible by encouraging the most fantastic initiatives, the most mind-boggling ideas. We have to transform the increasing scarcity of resources into a wealth of inventions. We may be at the dawn of an unheard-of revival of architecture, building construction, industry, and agriculture (here we might mention, more or less at random, the invention of solar-powered ships and aeroplanes, of dirigibles with transparent hulls, a hypersonic jet that will fly in the stratosphere, power produced by nuclear fusion, houses built on the model of termite's nests, constructing islands and floating cities, replacing meat by insects rich in protein, seeding the oceans with iron ore to grow planktonic algae, a huge green wall in Africa that would run from Djibouti to Senegal, solar-thermal power stations, small submarine nuclear power stations, etc.). Every new invention must strike the heart of human desire, elicit astonishment, and allow people to embark upon an unprecedented voyage. It is a *narrow door* (Luke XIII:24), but it is the door to salvation. We have to count on the genius of the human race, which is capable of overcoming its fears in order to improvise new solutions.

If a generous defence of the environment is to develop in the course of the next century, it will exist only as the servant of humans and nature in their mutual interaction and not as an advocate speaking through an entity called 'the planet'. The friends of the Earth have for too long been enemies of humanity; it is time for an ecology of admiration to replace an ecology of accusation.

Save the world, we hear everywhere: save it from capitalism, from science, from consumerism, from materialism. Above all, we have to save the world from its self-proclaimed saviours who brandish the threat of great chaos in order to impose their lethal impulses. Behind their clamour we must hear the will to demoralize us the better to enslave us. What is at stake here is the pleasure of living together on this planet that will survive us, whatever we do for it. We need trailblazers and stimulators, not killjoys disguised as prophets. We need new frontiers in order to cross them, not new prisons where we can stagnate. Humanity will emancipate itself only from above.

Notes

Introduction   The Return of Original Sin
1   I have discussed these two subjects in *Tears of the White Man: Compassion as Contempt*, trans. William R. Beer (New York: Free Press, 1986) and *The Tyranny of Guilt: An Essay on Western Masochism*, trans. Steven Rendall (Princeton: Princeton University Press, 2010).

Chapter 1   Give Me Back My Enemy
1   Here, I refer the reader to my book *La Mélancolie démocratique* (Paris: Seuil, 1990).
2   According to a reporter for *USA Today*, President George W. Bush was particularly enthusiastic about the prospects opened up by September 11: he saw in it an opportunity to present himself and his generation as the heralds of a vast project of cultural regeneration: 'Bush has told advisers that he believes confronting this enemy is a chance for him and his fellow baby boomers to refocus their lives and prove they have the same kind of valor and commitment their fathers showed in World War II.' Judy Keen, 'Same president, different man in the Oval Office,' *USA Today*, 29 October 2001.
3   Michel Serres, *Le Contrat naturel* (Paris: Champs, Essais, 1992), pp. 58–9. Ivan Illich had also essentially said that the thirty years of expansion in post-war Europe had had

the same destructive effect as the Second World War itself.

4 Yves Paccalet: 'I find it hard to understand how Darwinian evolution [. . .] could have favoured such an invasive, harmful, ill-spoken and short-lived species.' *L'humanité disparaîtra, bon débarras!* (Paris: Artaud, 2006).

5 Nicolas Hulot, *Pour un pacte écologique* (Paris: Calmann-Lévy, 2006).

6 'What should we do to eliminate suffering and disease? It's a wonderful idea but perhaps not altogether a beneficial one in the long run. If we try to implement it we may jeopardize the future of our species. [. . .] It's terrible to have to say this. World population must be stabilized and to do that we must eliminate 350,000 people per day. This is so horrible to contemplate that we shouldn't even say it.' *UNESCO Courier*, 1 November 1991. Quoted in Wikipedia, article 'Jacques Cousteau'.

7 In addition, opponents of speciesism demand a biospheric egalitarianism, granting the same rights to all living beings, animals, plants, trees, mountains. Naturally, they excoriate 'meat-eaters'.

8 Paul Taylor, *Respect for Nature: A Theory of Environmental Ethics (25th Anniversary Edition)* (Princeton: Princeton University Press, 2011), p. 115.

9 Quoted in Stéphane Ferret, *Deepwater Horizon* (Paris: Seuil, 2011), pp. 213–14.

10 Jared Diamond, *Collapse: How Societies Choose to Fail or to Succeed* (New York: Viking, 2005), p. 494.

11 François-Xavier Albouy, *Le Temps des catastrophes* (Paris: Descartes & Cie, 2002).

12 Serres, *Le Contrat naturel*, p. 136.

13 *Our Final Hour. A Scientist's Warning: How Terror, Error, and Environmental Disaster Threaten Humankind's Future in This Century on Earth and Beyond* (New York: Basic Books, 2003). Note the megalomania of this title, which makes human beings malevolent Titans capable of overturning the whole universe. Soon we'll be told that pollution bothers the eternal beatitude of the souls in Paradise.

14 George Monbiot, 'A self-fulfilling prophecy', *Guardian*, 17 March 2009.

15 The five earlier extinctions resulted from natural calamities, while the sixth is supposed to be due to human activity. The number of disappearances of species is said to be comparable, over a short period, to the five other massive extinctions, including that of the dinosaurs, that marked the Earth's geological past.

16 Quoted in Serge Latouche, *Le Pari de la décroissance* (Paris: Pluriel, 2010), new preface, pp. 10, 11.

17 Peter Barrett, director of the Antarctic Research Centre at the University of Victoria, New Zealand, 'Marsden Medal: Acceptance Comments and Notes', 17 November 2004.

18 Hervé Kempf, *Le Monde*, 14 October 2010.

19 Al Gore, interview in *L'Express*, 6 October 2006. Gore was vice president of the United States from 1996 to 2002, and wrote *An Inconvenient Truth: The Planetary Emergency of Global Warming and What We Can Do About It* (New York: Rodale, 2006). He is also the subject of a film with the same name.

20 Hans Jonas, *The Imperative of Responsibility: In Search of an Ethics for the Technological Age* (Chicago: University of Chicago Press, 1985).

21 Dominique Bourg and Kerry Whiteside, *Le Débat*, March–April 2011, no. 164, p. 169.

Chapter 2   Have the Courage to be Afraid

1 Roald Dahl, 'Genesis and catastrophe: a true story', in *Kiss Kiss* (New York: Knopf, 1960), p. 213.

2 Paul Virilio, *The Administration of Fear*, trans. Ames Hodges (Los Angeles: Semiotext(e), 2012), p. 55.

3 Jonas, *The Imperative of Responsibility*, pp. 26–7.

4 Ibid., p. 147.

5 See Mireille Delmas-Marty, *Libertés et sûreté dans un monde dangereux* (Paris: Seuil, 2010), pp. 135–7.

6 Dominique Bourg and Kerry Whiteside, *Vers une démocratie écologique* (Paris: Seuil, 2010), pp. 12–13.

7 Jean-Pierre Dupuy, *Pour un catastrophisme éclairé* (Paris: Seuil, 2002), p. 154.

8   Vittorio Hösle, *Philosophie de la crise écologique* (Marseille: Wildproject, 2009), p. 44.
9   Cf. Günther Anders on the nuclear holocaust: 'We are living in a period in which there are massive numbers of clean hands: the increase in people full of good will is considerable. We are going to die drowned in a flood of innocence. All around the man who is going to push the button and the movement of whose unbloodied finger will suffice to trigger the catastrophe will spread the ocean of the blood of those who, no matter how much they may have collaborated in it, will have absolutely not harboured nefarious designs and will not even have know that they collaborated.' *La Menace nucléaire: Considérations radicales sur l'âge atomiques* (Paris: Serpent à Plumes, 2006), pp. 277–8.
10 Hans Jonas, *Mortality and Morality: A Search for the Good After Auschwitz*, ed. Lawrence Vogel (Evanston, IL: Northwestern University Press, 1996), p. 103.
11 Quoted in Antoine Compagnon, *Les antimodernes* (Paris: Gallimard, 2005), p. 95.
12 Dupuy, *Pour un catastrophisme éclairé*, p. 91.
13 Michel Rocard, 24 March 2010, on the radio station France Inter: 'After all, we're not going to let the planet slowly become a frying pan in which life would become impossible. All right, it's slow. It will happen in ten or twelve generations, but it's so difficult to avoid that it would be better to begin early, out of prudence. In about ten years, concerning people who are slow in fighting against the climate, people will talk about a crime against humanity.' Quoted by Franck Nouchi, *Le Monde*, 26 March 2010.
14 Jean-Pierre Dupuy, 'De quoi l'avenir intellectuel sera-t-il fait?', *Le Débat*, 2010, p. 228. This nightmarish vision has no serious foundation. According to Cecilia Tacoli of the London-based International Institute for Environment and Development, 'There is no reason to think that environmental deterioration will lead to large international migratory movements. Migrants must not be seen as victims; on the contrary, migration is a rational strategy of economic development and adaptation to climate change.' Quoted in *Le Monde*, 8 February 2011.

15 Publicity material for the film *An Inconvenient Truth*, 2006.
16 Stéphane Foucart, *Le Monde*, 24 June 2011.
17 Bourg and Whiteside, *Vers une démocratie écologique*, p. 15.
18 I can't resist mentioning here the life of the British mathematician Alan Turing (1912–54), the founder of computer science and the brilliant decryptor of the Enigma encoding machine used by the Nazis. Persecuted after the war because of his homosexuality, Turing chose to commit suicide by eating an apple soaked in cyanide. According to his biographers, this method was modelled on the one used by the witch in the story of Snow White and the Seven Dwarfs, of which he was particularly fond. See Wikipedia, art. 'Alan Turing'.
19 On the vogue of shipwreck stories in Holland, a country that is always threatened by the sea and the rupture of its dikes, see Simon Schama, *The Embarassment of Riches* (New York: Knopf, 1987), p. 30: 'The Dutch publishers who turned out this kind of epic were the first entrepreneurs of armchair calamity.'
20 See Keith Thomas, *Man and the Natural World: Changing Attitudes in England, 1500–1800* (London: Allen Lane, 1983).
21 Jean Starobinski, *L'Invention de la liberté*, reprint (Paris: Gallimard, 2006), pp. 68–9.
22 Robert Macfarlane, *Mountains of the Mind* (New York: Pantheon, 2003), pp. 99, 71.
23 A film by John Hillcoat, with Viggo Mortensen, based on the fine eponymous novel by Cormac McCarthy, 2009.
24 Philippe Ariès, *Essais sur l'histoire de la mort en Occident, du Moyen Age à nos jours* (Paris: Points Seuil, 1975), p. 25.
25 George Romero, *The Night of the Living Dead*, 1968.
26 Anders, *La Menace nucléaire*, p. 105.
27 See Andrew Lakoff, *Esprit*, March–April 2008, p. 106.
28 I refer here to Marc Godin's excellent study, *Gore: Autopsie d'un cinéma* (Paris: Éditions du Collectionneur, 1994).

29   Michel Rocard, Dominique Bourg, and Floran Augagneur, 'Le genre humain menacé', *Le Monde*, 3 April 2011.

30   Jean-Jacques Rousseau, *Discours sur l'origine de l'inégalité*, Part II (Paris: Garnier-Flammarion, 1971), p. 205.

31   René Guénon, *La Crise du monde moderne* (Paris: Gallimard, collection Idées, 1974), pp. 90–1.

32   For Jacques Grinevald, a philosopher of science, 'Original Sin' is to be found in the universe of the engineer connected with the revolution inaugurated by Sadi Carnot, a French physician who laid the foundations for the Second Law of Thermodynamics and who died in 1832. Engineers are guilty of having invented water wheels, thermal power stations, and turbines! (*Le Monde Magazine*, 2, 1 January 2011.)

33   Rocard et al., 'Le genre humain menacé'. The sentence itself is strange: how can a threat be transformed into a desirable promise? One does away with a menace; one doesn't transform it!

34   Bourg and Whiteside, *Vers une démocratie écologique*, p. 9.

35   'We have here an inversion of Descartes's principle of doubt. In order to ascertain the indubitable truth we should, according to Descartes, equate everything doubtful with the demonstrably false. Here, on the contrary, we are told to treat, for the purposes of decision, the doubtful but possible as if it were certain, when it is of a certain kind.' Jonas, *The Imperative of Responsibility*, p. 37.

36   Dupuy, *Pour un catastrophisme éclairé*, p. 63.

37   Alan Weisman, *The World Without Us* (New York: Dunne/St Martin's Press, 2007).

Chapter 3   Blackmailing Future Generations

1   Leon Festinger, Henry W. Riecken, and Stanley Schatchter, *When Prophecy Fails* (Minneapolis: University of Minnesota Press, 1956; reprint London: Pinter and Martin, 2008).

2   Ibid., p. 132.

3 On the parallel rise in well-being and the culture of lament, I refer to my essay *La Tentation de l'innocence* (Paris: Grasset, 1995). On this subject, Bruno Tertrais, in *L'Apocalypse n'est pas pour demain: Pour en finir avec le catastrophisme* (Paris: Denoël, 2011), develops excellent statistical arguments regarding the decrease in poverty, the so-called 'population bomb', and the end of wars.

4 Anders, *La Menace nucléaire*, pp. 317–18.

5 *L'Express*, 20 April 2011.

6 'Every catastrophe has three essential parameters: its realization, the likelihood that it will be repeated, and the maximum extent it can attain.' Albouy, *Le Temps des catastrophes*, p. 71.

7 Hannah Arendt, *The Promise of Politics*, ed. Jerome Kohn (New York: Schocken, 2005).

8 Jonas, *The Imperative of Responsibility*, p. 41.

9 Émilie Sébileau, quoted by Delmas-Marty, *Libertés et sûreté dans un monde dangereux*, pp. 172–3.

10 This is the epistemological argument that Jean de Kervasdoué opposes to the principle of precaution: 'To assert that one can be capable of protecting a group from a phenomenon whose nature we do not know is absurd, but claiming that one can do it has become a political necessity.' *La peur est au-dessus de nos moyens* (Paris: Plon, 2011), p. 220.

11 Bourg and Whiteside, *Vers une démocratie écologique*, p. 47.

12 Jean-Pierre Dupuy, *Le Monde*, 24–5 October 2010.

13 Anders, *La Menace nucléaire*, p. 100.

14 Martin Buber, *Reden über das Judentum* (Frankfurt, 1923); Eng. trans.: *On Judaism* (New York: Schocken, 1996), pp. 118–19.

15 See the fundamental book by Norman Cohn, *The Pursuit of the Millennium* (London: Secker and Warburg, 1957).

16 'Our apocalyptic passion has no objective other than to prevent the apocalypse. We are apocalyptical only in order to be wrong,' said, for example, Günther Anders in 1960 (*La Menace nucléaire*, p. 259). One may have doubts about this declared humility.

17 Diamond, *Collapse*.
18 Luc Mary, *Le mythe de la fin du monde* (Paris: Éditions Trajectoire, 2009). Source: *Journal du Dimanche*, 7 November 2009.
19 Hergé's *L'Étoile mystérieuse* (Paris: Casterman, 1947). Pétainism is in two ways the precursor of a certain kind of ecology: by its assertion that 'the Earth doesn't lie', and by its repeated appeal for collective penitence. Unfortunately for our penitents, the only regime in France that has adopted this motto is that of collaboration. The connections between ecology and fascism have often been emphasized and would be worth a separate study.
20 Jonas, *The Imperative of Responsibility*, p. 120.

Chapter 4   The Last Avatar of Prometheus?
1 On Piranesi, see Starobinski, *L'Invention de la liberté*, pp. 174–5.
2 Ivan Illich, *Némésis médicale* (Paris: Seuil, 1975), pp. 203–4. In Greek mythology, Nemesis is the goddess of vengeance.
3 Alain Finkielkraut offers a fine commentary on this decision in *Nous autres, modernes* (Paris: Ellipses, 2005), pp. 353ff. On 26 March 2011, the 'Earth Hour' operation plunged 134 countries into darkness for an hour 'to help the world see the light', according to Ban Ki-moon, the secretary-general of the UN. In Paris, the cathedral of Notre Dame, the Garnier and Bastille operas, and even the Eiffel Tower were extinguished for a few minutes.
4 'In its essence, agriculture is now a motorized food industry, the same thing as the production of corpses in the gas chambers and the extermination camps, the same thing as blockades and the reduction of countries to famine, the same thing as the construction of hydrogen bombs.' Quoted in Philippe Lacoue-Labarthe, *La fiction du politique* (Paris: Christian Bourgois, 1987), p. 58.
5 *Idea for a Universal History with a Cosmopolitan Purpose*.
6 François Ewald, *Encyclopædia Universalis*, 2001, art. 'Risque technologique'.

7   See Thomas, *Man and the Natural World.*
8   According to the American Geological Institute, the number of earthquakes has been relatively stable over the past century, close to the prediction of eighteen per year that exceed 7 on the Richter scale. If there is a greater number of victims, that is because high-risk zones are more heavily populated than they used to be. Not to mention that in the age of Twitter and smart phones, the media noise about catastrophes is exploding. Some people will nonetheless point out that over the past thirty years, the number of devastating earthquakes (over 8 on the Richter scale) seems to be increasing: four in the 1980s, six in the 1990s, and thirteen in the decade following 2000. Stephen Gao, a geologist at the University of Missouri, recognizes that there has been a relative increase since the 1990s, but there is no consensus as to why this is. One suggestion is that it could be due to simple temporary variations in pressure in the lithosphere (source: *20 Minutes*, 15 March 2011).
9   Charles Onians, *The Independent*, 20 March 2000.
10 Anthony Giddens and Martin Rees, 'Open letter on climate change', *Huffington Post*, 22 September 2010.
11 Cohn, *The Pursuit of the Millennium*, p. 136.
12 'Global warming is global cooling.'
13 It has to be hoped that global warming will soon be confirmed: if the climatologists' simulations turned out to be mistaken, that would be a genuine symbolic catastrophe, years of indoctrination invalidated. But after all, if we had the Riviera's climate in Brittany, grape vines growing along the Thames, or palm trees in Sweden, who would complain?
14 Agnès Sinaï, 'Fukushima ou la fin de l'anthropocène. Sortir d'urgence de l'inanité de notre mode de croissance', *Le Monde*, 19 March 2011.
15 Jean-Pierre Dupuy, 'Une catastrophe monstre', *Le Monde*, 20–1 March 2011.
16 Hervé Kempf, *Le Monde*, 17–18 January 2010.
17 Naomi Klein, *The Shock Doctrine: The Rise of Disaster Capitalism* (New York: Picador, 2008).

18 Latouche, *Le Pari de la décroissance*, p. 224. Latouche's work is amusing in that it synthesizes in a few hundred pages all the foolishness of radical ecology.
19 Harald Welzer, *Le Monde*, 31 October 2009.
20 Among the many studies on Katrina, there is a good synthesis in *Cybergeo, revue européenne de géographie*, no. 353, 12 October 2006. See also the excellent TV series *Treme* on the survivors' determination to reconstruct their city and return to it.
21 Trailer for Jacques Perrin's film *Océans*, February 2011.
22 Ulrich Beck, *Risk Society: Towards a New Modernity* (London: Sage, 1992), p. 31.
23 I borrow these distinctions from Ferret, *Deepwater Horizon*, pp. 124–5. Animal ethics is represented by Peter Singer and Tom Regan, biocentric ethics by Albert Schweitzer and Paul Taylor, ecospheric ethics by Aldo Leopold, Arne Naess, and John Baird Callicott.
24 As has been noted by Dominique Lecourt, *L'Âge de la peur* (Paris: Bayard Presse, 2009), pp. 136–7.
25 Carol J. Adams, 'Anima, animus, animal', *Cahiers antispécistes*, no 3, April 1992, quoted in Jean-Baptiste Jeangène Vilmer, *L'Éthique animale* (Paris: PUF, 2011).
26 See Ferret, *Deepwater Horizon*, who wonders how well founded these propositions are (pp. 180ff.).
27 On this point, see Luc Ferry's enlightening demonstration, *Le Nouvel Ordre écologique* (Paris: Grasset, 1993), as well as Dominique Bourg, *L'Homme artifice* (Paris: Le Débat, Gallimard, 1996), pp. 332–3.
28 Ferret, *Deepwater Horizon*, p. 32.
29 *The Economist*, 2 June 2011, 'A man-made world'. This is still a hypothesis.
30 I thank Jean-François Braunstein, professor of the philosophy of science at the Sorbonne, for this information. This ambition provides the plot for Jules Verne's novel *Sans dessus dessous* (*The Purchase of the North Pole or Topsy-Turvy*), in which a group of American industrialists undertakes to straighten up the Earth's axis in order to gain access to the mineral resources of the Far North. In *Paradise Lost*, Milton made the tilt of the Earth's access a consequence of Original Sin (see Michel Serres, *Jules Verne ou l'enchantement du monde* (conversations

with Jean-Paul Dekiss) [Paris: Le Pommier, 2010], p. 158).

31 Jane Kramer, *Lone Patriot* (New York: Vintage, 2002).

Chapter 5   Nature, a Cruel Stepmother or a Victim?

1   Quoted in *Le Temps de la responsabilité*, ed. Frédéric Lenoir (Paris: Fayard, 1991), p. 77. According to the *New York Times*, April 1992, this letter is in fact a forgery written in 1971 by a screenwriter with ecological sensibilities.

2   E.O. Wilson, *The Diversity of Life* (New York: Norton, 1992), cited in Dominique Bourg, *Nature et technique*. Paris: Hatier, 1997), pp. 38–9.

3   Serres, *Le Contrat naturel*.

4   Ibid., p. 187.

5   Ibid., p. 188.

6   Gaston Bachelard, *La Formation de l'esprit scientifique* (Paris: Vrin, 1938).

7   'Christ shed his blood for kine and horses . . . as well as for men,' said William Bowling, a member of a Protestant sect in Kent, in 1646. Quoted in Thomas, *Man and the Natural World*, p. 139. For Martin Luther, venomous pests and flesh-eating beasts are the result of our sins. Once the Last Judgment has been pronounced, they will become 'pretty, loveable, and tender, and little dogs with golden skins and bejewelled coats will gambol about'. Luther, *Table Talk*, quoted in Jean Delumeau, *Histoire de la peur en Occident* (Paris: Pluriel, 1978), p. 271.

8   Thomas, *Man and the Natural World*.

9   On trials of animals, see Ferry's very convincing analysis in *Le Nouvel Ordre écologique*.

10 The anecdote is reported in Thomas, *Man and the Naural World*, p. 128.

11 On this, see Elisabeth de Fontenay's pertinent reflections in her book *Le Silence des bêtes* (Paris: Fayard, 1998).

12 Peter Singer, 'Heavy petting', *Nerve Magazine*, March/April 2001.

13 See also the book *When Species Meet* (Minneapolis: University of Minnesota Press, 2007), by Donna Haraway, an American feminist who studies her

post-human relations with her bitch, Madame Cayenne Pepper, whom she French kisses.
14 Thomas, *Man and the Natural World.*
15 Étienne Barillier, *Contre le nouvel obscurantisme* (Paris: Éditions Zoé; Geneva: L'Hebdo, 1995), pp. 71–2.
16 Stephen Jay Gould, *Eight Little Piggies* (New York: Vintage, 2007), p. 49.

Chapter 6   Science in the Age of Suspicion
1 Beck, *Risk Society*, pp. 72–3.
2 See, for example, the website ASV Végétarisme.ch., according to which world meat production requires an enormous consumption of water and massive deforestation (70 per cent of the deforestation in the Amazon basin is attributed to pasturing livestock). Soybeans, a major component of animal feed, are cultivated to the detriment of other cereals, and the antibiotics frequently administered to cattle end up in the milk and meat they produce. Liquid manure and animal excrements pollute our waters and destroy trees. The conclusion: 'The fewer animal products we consume, the more we are acting in favour of the climate.'
3 Cf. Jonathan Safran Foer's recent book *Eating Animals* (New York: Little, Brown, 2009). In addition to vegetarians who do not eat meat, we find 'dietary vegans' who also abstain from fish, milk, cream, and yogurt, and even 'environmental vegans' who refuse to wear leather, wool, or silk, or to eat honey produced by beekeepers. You can't go much further than that.
4 *Le Monde*, 2 December 2010, a study commissioned by the 'Générations futures' association and the journal *Health and Environment Alliance* in collaboration with the 'Environnement santé' network and WWF France.
5 See the website *www.eoliennesatoutprix.be/.*
6 François Ewald, *Au risque d'innover* (Paris: Autrement, 2009).
7 'Entretiens avec Guy Lacroix', *Terminal*, Winter 1993, p. 123. 'Nous allons vers des Tchernobyls informatiques', in Bourg, *L'Homme artifice*, p. 268.
8 For France alone, according to the statistics for 2011 provided by the Ministry of National Education,

undergraduate programmes in science attract only 11 per cent of students compared with 24 per cent in 1996 and 17 per cent in 2002. Between 2002 and 2009, the number of students in basic science programmes declined by 5.9 per cent, that of students in biological sciences by 9.4 per cent.

9   Beck, *Risk Society*.
10   In a 2001 television interview with Karl Zéro, Bové, a fervent opponent of Israeli colonialism, in which he saw an emanation of the liberal serpent, accused Mossad of burning French synagogues in order to foment trouble between Jews and Arabs. He later apologized for having perhaps wounded some people's sensibilities with his words. A little related question: who benefited from the tactics adopted by the activists who destroyed the grapevines? During the night of 14 August 2010, teams of volunteers deliberately destroyed plots planted with genetically modified grapevines that were being used by the National Institute for Agricultural Research in Colmar, Alsace, for the purpose of testing products intended to fight fanleaf, a widespread viral disease affecting vineyards. The damage done thus put an end to the research being done there. The result: the French GMO industry has been destroyed by the Confédération Paysanne's forceful interventions, which has thus become – perhaps involuntarily – the accomplice of the powerful firm Monsanto.
11   See Étienne Klein's illuminating article 'La science en question', *Le Débat*, April–May 2004, pp. 148–9.
12   Lecourt, *L'Âge de la peur*, p. 64.
13   Clifford D. Simak, *City* (New York: Gnome Press, 1952).
14   'Des gaz à effet de serre dans mon assiette', Réseau Action Climat-France, 2009.
15   Latouche, *Le Pari de la décroissance*, p. 221. The obsession with packaging is a constant among ecologists. In the 1970s, André Gorz had already made it his hobby horse.
16   Bill McKibben, 'Small world: Why one town stays unplugged', *Harper's*, December 2003, quoted in Latouche, *Le Pari de la décroissance*, p. 221.

17 Benoît Rittaud, *Le Mythe climatique* (Paris: Seuil, 2010), p. 176. In this excellent work, the mathematician Rittaud calls the pseudoscience attached to climatology 'climatomancy: an art of divination seeking to deduce from human behaviour the climatic future of the Earth, with the goal of prescribing penitential acts for everyone', p. 169.

18 Sigmund Freud, *Introductory Lectures on Psycho-Analysis (Part III) (Standard Edition*, Vol. 16), ed. and trans. James Strachey (London: Hogarth Press, 1966), pp. 284–5.

19 On this subject, see the enlightening discussion in Ferret, *Deepwater Horizon*, pp. 273ff.

20 According to the European Space Agency, which notes that this does not necessarily reflect a long-term tendency.

21 See Bourg, *Nature et technique*, p. 54.

22 On this subject, Vilmer, *L'Éthique animale*, pp. 56–8.

23 Using perhaps the process of 'terraformation' already envisaged for Mars: 'creating a greenhouse effect [. . .], implanting genetically modified bacteria capable of transforming the planet's carbon dioxide into oxygen, melting the polar icecaps, and re-creating oceans' – all processes described by a science-fiction author, Kim Stanley Robinson. Cf. Jean Staune, *La Science en otage* (Paris: Presses de la Renaissance, 2010), pp. 334–5.

24 According to the brilliant reading provided by Serres, *Jules Verne ou l'enchantement du monde*, pp. 60–1.

25 Voltaire, *Mélanges* (Paris: Gallimard (Pléïade), 1961), pp. 304ff.

26 Rousseau to Voltaire, 18 August 1756, in *Oeuvres complètes de J.-J. Rousseau*, Vol. 7 (Paris: Hachette, 1864), p. 36.

27 See Albouy, *Le Temps des catastrophes*, pp. 30–2.

28 See Stanislaw Lem's science fiction classic, 'The World as Cataclysm', in *One Human Minute*, trans. Catherine S. Leach (San Diego: Harcourt Brace Jovanovich, 1986), p. 98.

Chapter 7 Humanity on a Strict Diet

1 Latouche, *Le Pari de la décroissance*, p. 56. Note the discreet allusion to the 'banality of evil', which refers to

Nazism and suggests implicitly that our democratic societies are hardly better than the Third Reich. Ah! How easy the amalgamation is . . .

2 Ibid., pp. 53–4.

3 Denis Bayon, *Décroissance économique: Vers une société de sobriété écologique*, *www.decroissance.org*, quoted in Latouche, *Le Pari de la décroissance*, p. 60.

4 Gilles Châtelet, *Vivre et penser comme des porcs* (Paris: Gallimard, Folio, 1998). The author, a critic of liberal counter-reformation, attacks, among other things, 'petro-nomadism' and 'Pétainism on wheels', that is, the cult of the car.

5 Theodor W. Adorno, 'Extracts from *Minima Moralia: Reflections from Damaged Life*', in Clive Cazeaux (ed.), *The Continental Aesthetics Reader* (London: Routledge, 2000), p. 240.

6 Rousseau, *Discours sur l'origine de l'inégalité*, p. 216.

7 Yves Cochet, *Le Point*, 24 March 2011.

8 Mathis Wackeragel, 'Il nostro planeta si sta esaurendo', in Andrea Masullo (ed.), *Economia e ambient* (Bologna: EMI, 2005), quoted in Latouche, *Le Pari de la décroissance*, p. 134.

9 Robert E. Lane, *The Loss of Happiness in Market Democracies* (New Haven: Yale University Press, 2000), quoted by Latouche, *Le Pari de la décroissance*, p. 80. The argument is untenable. There is no instrument for measuring the happiness that is not a fixed quantity but an impalpable feeling. The author confuses well-being and happiness, but above all it is our conception of happiness that has changed over the last half-century; we have made it an essential condition of our success. We make ourselves unhappy about not being happy.

10 Hervé Kempf, *Le Monde*, 28–9 June 2009.

11 Hervé Kempf, *Le Monde*, 30 June 2010.

12 Ivan Illich, *La Convivialité* (Paris: Seuil, 1973), p. 572.

13 Latouche, *Le Pari de la décroissance*, pp. 214–15.

14 François Brune, *De l'idéologie, aujourd'hui* (Paris: Parangon, 2005).

15 Bruno Clémentin and Vincent Cheynet, *Objectif décroissance* (Paris: Parangon, 2003), p. 103.

16 Brune, *De l'idéologie, aujourd'hui*, p. 103.

17 Harald Welzer, *Le Monde*, 26 March 2011.

18 Latouche, *Le Pari de la décroissance*, p. 161.
19 Sylvia Pérez-Vitoria, *Les paysans sont de retour*, quoted in Latouche, *Le Pari de la décroissance*, pp. 95–6.
20 See Cohn, *The Pursuit of the Millennium*, pp. 195–6.
21 The father of the movement to reverse growth, Pierre Rabhi, a recluse who lives in the Cevennes mountains in southern France, has been nicknamed 'the local Gandhi'. One could be forgiven for thinking that Gandhi had a quite different moral and political stature. . .
22 Dominique Bourg, *Le Point*, 24 March 2011.
23 Conceived in Britain, the Transition movement notes the 'energy descent' (Rob Hopkins), which it sees as an immense opportunity to rethink our ways of life. It advocates reversing growth, relocalization, locavorism, the purchasing of local products.
24 Latouche, *Le Pari de la décroissance*, p. 240.
25 Ivan Illich, *La Perte des sens* (Paris: Fayard, 2004).
26 Latouche, *Le Pari de la décroissance*, p. viii.
27 Paul Ariès, *Décroissance ou barbarie* (Paris: Éditions Golias, 2005), quoted in Latouche, *Le Pari de la décroissance*, p. 41.

Chapter 8 The Poverty of Maceration
1 Quoted in Dominique Nora, *Les pionniers de l'or vert: Ils inventent le XXIe siècle* (Paris: Grasset, 2009), p. 305.
2 Ibid., pp. 6ff.
3 François Dagnaud, assistant to the mayor of Paris, regarding the composting bins installed at the base of some apartment buildings. Quoted by Iegor Gran in his book *L'Écologie en bas de chez moi* (Paris: POL, 2011), p. 148.
4 In the Middle Ages, *avaritia* was a passion greedy for life and beings, and not the petty stinginess that we have castigated since Molière. See Ariès, *Essais sur l'histoire de la mort en Occident*, p. 82.
5 Ibid., p. 83.
6 Olivier Guez, 'La Révolution verte version californienne', *Le Monde Magazine*, 28 August 2010.
7 *Le Nouvel Observateur*, special issue on ecology, 3–9 December 2009, focused on Daniel Cohn-Bendit.

8   Quoted by Gran, *L'Écologie en bas de chez moi*, p. 42.
9   Quoted in 'La Vie meilleure, mode d'emploi', *Courrier International*, Autumn 2009, p. 67.
10 Guez, 'La Révolution verte version californienne'.
11 Colin Beavan, *No Impact Man* (New York: Picador, 2010), p. 14.
12 Michael Pollan, *The Omnivore's Dilemma*, quoted in Beavan, *No Impact Man*, p. 126. Brackets added by Beavan.
13 Beavan, *No Impact Man*, pp. 93ff.
14 Ibid.
15 International Washable Diaper Week (Semaine internationale de la couche lavable, SICL) organized by the Bulle de coton association. *Economag, le gratuit des écolos pratiques*, no. 22, March–April 2011.
16 All sources cited in an article by Joel Garreau, 'Environmentalism as religion', *The New Atlantis*, Summer 2010.
17 'People [. . .] will break their ties with super-efficient transportation as soon as they are able to appreciate the limited area in which they move and fear having to leave home.' Ivan Illich, *Energie et équité* (Paris: Seuil, 1973), p. 43.
18 Daniel Defoe, *Robinson Crusoe* (Oxford: Oxford University Press [World's Classics], 2008), p. 57.
19 Michel Tournier, *Friday, or the Other Island*, trans. Norman Denny (London: Collins, 1969).
20 Gilles Deleuze, 'Michel Tournier and the World Without Others', in *The Logic of Sense*, trans. Mark Lester (London: Continuum, 2004), pp. 341–58.

Chapter 9   The Noble Savage in the Lucerne
1   David Graeber, *Fragments of an Anarchist Anthropology* (Chicago: Prickly Paradigm Press, 2004), pp. 53–4.
2   Rousseau, *Discours sur l'origine de l'inégalité*, pp. 168–9.
3   Theodore J. Kaczynski, *The Road to Revolution* (Vevey, Switzerland: Xenia, 2008), p. 36 and 104. Kaczynski acutely criticizes the neo-primitivist myths promoted by a certain branch of the American left, but in his rage against techno-scientism he himself produces others.

4   On the appearance of new nativist metaphysics in post-colonial thought, see the illuminating work by Jean-Loup Amselle, *Rétrovolutions* (Paris: Stock, 2010).

5   Brune, *De l'idéologie, aujourd'hui*, p. 165.

6   Yves Cochet, *Pétrole Apocalypse* (Paris: Fayard, 2005), pp. 166–7.

7   *New York Times Magazine*, 27 February 2011.

8   Jean-Marie Gustave Le Clézio, interviewed by François Armanet regarding Native Americans, *Le Nouvel Observateur*, Summer 2006.

9   Jean-Marie Gustave Le Clézio, *Haï* (Geneva: Skira, 1971), p. 11.

10   See Diamond, *Collapse*.

11   According to Wikipedia, in 2010 Palestinian militants disguised themselves as Na'vis in order to protest against the wall being constructed by the Israelis, while elsewhere other communities drew on this film to protest the military-industrial complex in China, Borneo, and the Amazon Basin. *Avatar* has become the cult film of the NGO 'Survival', which is concerned with the fate of oppressed tribes such as the Guarini, the Adivasi, and the pygmies.

12   See Thomas, *Man and the Natural World*.

13   Quoted by Dominique Nora, who describes these movements in detail in *Les pionniers de l'or vert*, p. 81.

14   J.P. Géné, 'Un potager dans la ville', *Le Monde Magazine*, 1 January 2011.

15   Jean-Marie Pelt, interviewed by Frédéric Lenoir in *Le Temps de la responsabilité*, preface by Paul Ricoeur (Paris: Fayard, 1991), p. 91.

16   De Kervasdoué, *La peur est au-dessus de nos moyens*, p. 11.

17   Bruno Tertrais provides a very convincing demonstration of this in *L'Apocalypse n'est pas pour demain*.